Echoes from the Sandhills

Sincerely
Franklin C. Jackson

Home Is Where the Heart Is

By Bernice Koch

I've wandered over hill and dale;
I've crossed the great divide;
I've walked along the beaches
of the oceans far and wide.

I've ridden on the prairies;
and I've walked beneath the pine.
I have lived in farming countries
Where the crops all look so fine.

But the place that seems like home to me
Where I was born and raised
Is the Sandhills of Nebraska;
That's the place I've always praised.

You can stand upon the hill top
With the valley far below
And wonder at its beauty,
For God has made it so.

The air is pure and fresh and clean
And you can see so far;
No smog to clutter up the air
No matter where you are.

The cattle grazing far and wide,
A sight beyond compare;
A ranch house in the valley
With lots of room to spare.

The place is next to Heaven;
And I always say a prayer,
To thank God for that lovely place,
He's always with you there.

Reprinted from the *Grant County News,* by permission of the author.

Echoes from the Sandhills

Franklin C. Jackson

WORD SERVICES ● LINCOLN, NEBRASKA

First Edition
First Printing

Published by

WORD SERVICES, 3706 N.W. 51 Street, Lincoln, Nebraska 68524

Dedicated to my mother,
Catherine Jackson,
who helped with the memories,
and to my dear wife,
Elsie Lee Jackson,
who put in many hours of hard work helping me
and typing this up

Contents

"Hello There"

By Jack Moreland

ON A SANDHILLS RANCH, 46 miles southeast of Gordon, dwells a sturdy couple who celebrated their Golden Wedding two years ago and who are still active and in good health. It is Mr. and Mrs. Carl Jackson of whom we are now making this narrative report, and we are sure you readers will be interested to know how they have met such challenges as came along.

David Jackson and his wife, Mary Shipley Jackson, were the grandparents of Carl. David Jackson bought up trail herds and moved them to states north of his native Texas. The cattle were then sold and the money used to buy more cattle for the next drive. Some were sold to military forts, some to the government for Indian issue, and some to the ranchers along the way who were accumulating their own herds. Occasionally he trailed horses northward instead of steers.

Three sons, John, Frank, and Charley, and two daughters, Eva Jackson Richer and Anna Jackson Lambert, completed the David Jackson family. They are now all deceased.

Frank and Nellie Jackson, whom some of the older residents of Merriman and Martin, South Dakota, will remember, were the parents of Carl, who was born at Cascade, South Dakota, Bess (Mrs. Lee Pratt, of Sheridan, Oregon), and Ruth (Mrs. Charles Cody, of Hood River, Oregon)—all of whom are living. The parents passed away many years ago.

First published in *The Nebraska Cattleman,* February 1962; reprinted by courtesy of the editor.

The Frank Jackson family lived for some time in western South Dakota not far from an inland post office named Folsom. They ran some cattle along Indian Creek Basin not long after the present century was ushered in. Carl spent his vacations in his father's camp. His playmates were the Frank Hart children. Frank was mentioned in Will Spindler's latest book. Sheep Mountain was one of the local landmarks. Near the Wyoming line it was all open range. When Carl was nine there was no railroad and no town of Scenic. When he was sixteen they moved over into Wyoming for awhile.

Carl Jackson and one of his horses. Dad has told me many times how hard this horse could buck.

"Rep" for His Father

There were some large cattle outfits with headquarters in and around Hot Springs. These held spring and fall roundups and Carl said they sometimes worked most of the summer. For the next three years after he was sixteen, Carl rode as his father's "rep," with a string of 13 horses. He sometimes tired out four or five of them in one day if the going was tough.

The roundups were planned and the range foremen were appointed in the early spring meeting. When the wagons moved out a dozen or so riders would cover the territory for each of them. The open range extended from the Bad River to the Missouri. The system followed was to bunch the cattle on a flat where there was room to work. Riders would go into the herd and bring out beef bearing the brand or brands they were responsible for. There were supposed to be enough men and boys left to hold the herd together in a bunch but the cowboys all wanted to go in and cut out cattle, often leaving the holding riders short-handed.

It was the purpose of the roundup to work each owner's beef close to their home range so they could be driven on to market shipping points. Arrangements were often made to make up loads of more than one brand. When these loads reached their destination the commission firm would sort, sell, and mail separate checks to the different owners. So many cattle were billed to the John Clay Commission Co., that Carl said he was in his teens before he realized that there were other firms engaged in the same business.

In these roundups there might be more "Reps" than big outfit cowboys. Some rode clear through the shipping season. others dropped out as they reached their territory to be replaced by riders from farther beyond. About once every two weeks a drive would start for the nearest railroad.

There was a Reservation fence on the state line that was supposed to keep white ranchers' cattle separated from those of Indian owners. There was always more grass on the reservation side so the big outfits would sometimes send riders to cut the fence in the draws to let their cattle in on good feed ahead of the roundup. Later they would try to get the cattle out and back to the main herd when the roundup came along.

Detained by Police

Carl Jackson and a rider by the name of Alfred Polmon were sent in to bring out a bunch of white owners' cattle and were caught by Indian Police. There was nothing to do but go along with them for a hearing at Pine Ridge. The "court" turned them loose but they were hungry, without money, and a long way from their outfit. Fortunately, Corb Morrison, owner of the Six L outfit, had made arrangements at White Clay so that his riders and probably others were staked to a good meal or two before starting back outside the reservation fence.

In 1908 Carl Jackson and Catherine Mahoney were married and set up housekeeping in the Hot Springs vicinity. Three years later they decided to leave the Black Hills because of the drouth conditions there, and filed on a Kinkaid homestead, forty-seven miles southeast of Gordon. They lived on the homestead for eight years, then sold out. That land is now owned by their son-in-law and daughter, the Wallace Adams.

The sale of the Kinkaid involved 4,500 accumulated acres. They had made considerable progress in the cattle business since the day in 1911 when Catherine got off the train in Gordon where she was met by Carl who had driven his wagon all the way from the Black Hills, bringing everything he owned including some cattle to stock the homestead.

A Tribute to My Parents and All Sandhills Pioneers

By Mrs. Wallace Adam

I HAPPENED TO BE with my parents sometime ago when Mr. J. J. Moreland conversed with them about doing a feature article for *The Nebraska Cattleman* magazine. He suggested that perhaps I would do the article. I was indeed flattered but know that my little writing attempts will never equal writings of Mr. Moreland, but since he suggested I might like to contribute a little something, I considered it a great opportunity to offer a word of praise to my wonderful parents; to the Morelands and all other Sandhill pioneers who have struggled for survival a half century or so in these old Sandhills. Theirs has been a difficult life, but where can you find people any happier or who wear a bigger smile than these fine folks?

We now have the folks' homestead and live not far from the ranch where the family grew up. People think we are from a forgotten world when we tell them we are 20 miles from the nearest improved road. The folks raised us four children in considerable isolation. It was perhaps worse because they were so far from even a graveled road and the cars just weren't what they might have been in those days. Oh, it was great to hear Dad coming with the freight wagon. We would run down the trail to meet him. We used to have one room where we would pile winter supplies—50 lb. sacks of flour, 300

First published in *The Nebraska Cattleman,* February 1962; reprinted by courtesy of the editor.

lbs. of sugar and such, and now if you buy supplies for even a month or two the clerk wonders if perhaps you haven't "flipped."

One of these pioneer abilities that I will never cease marveling at was their effective doctoring ability. Nowadays our children receive all their shots as per scheduled—get a shot of penicillin and everything is fine! Mother was always doctoring cuts (her rabbit ear bandages were beautiful), gashes, colds and such and Dad's knife was always in top shape for cutting out slivers. He could wrap a cut or sprain or even a broken bone professionally. The folks didn't even have a telephone connection with a telephone for 40 years. Now we have a telephone connection with a telephone than can at least call a doctor for us if we need immediate consultation. All pioneer parents have this doctoring ability and I think it is marvelous. They are wonderful people!

How these folks got all "us kids" educated will always be a mystery to me. We have trouble getting a teacher, and complain about everything. They had as much trouble finding good teachers, getting children to school, but it was just part of their job.

I believe I know what carried these fine folks through —their sense of humor and ability to enjoy themselves regardless. We'd do well to follow their example. We have everything; they had nothing. One of my favorite stories is about one time Dad had roped a yearling for doctoring. With nothing better to do, Mother was right there (I admire that family togetherness. Why don't we have it nowadays?) and felt quite brave since Dad had the critter roped. The critter was slightly "snuffy" and about that time Dad hollered, "Look out, Katy, he got loose!" Mother says she ran and ran like she never ran before. They were out in the open and quite some distance from the buildings. She says she could see she couldn't possibly reach protection as she couldn't possibly take another step and decided the critter might just as well hit her and have it over with. She stopped, the critter stopped. Dad's rope was still on it!!! He was just letting her get a little exercise. Mother laughs about it now but I'm not so sure it was so funny that day.

To Mother and Dad, to all our dear pioneer friends and neighbors, may I say we admire you? We probably forget to say so or don't say so often enough, but we think you are wonderful and owe you a great debt of gratitude for showing us the Sandhills are hard to battle, but also hard to beat when it comes to looking for a place to call home.

In closing I would like to reveal a little family secret— the answer to the question, "Where did your parents meet?" Mother was visiting with her sister and family and was as handy with a hammer as the average (or better) man.   Mother was helping out by doing a shingling job for the family. What was she shingling? Nowadays you know, people have so many rooms and a bath but this family had so many rooms and a house at the end of the path. It was this little house out back that Mother was shingling. Here came this dashing cowboy gallently riding his horse down the trail. Indeed, Mother was embarrassed but she couldn't possibly make a getaway because Dad was there before she realized anyone was around. It must have been love at first sight because they were soon married. I don't know if it was their wedding day or just a courtship buggy trip, but on a little drive one time, Dad reached out of the buggy and picked some cedar berries. He insisted Mother try them —they were so delicious and she had never seen any. He also took some—"My, they were delicious." Mother didn't want to be rude but didn't like to say they were horrid when Dad thought they were so good. Dad gave her some more. Polite or not, Mother had to refuse. Try as hard as she could she just couldn't down them. It wasn't until years later Mother found out he spit his berries out—I can just imagine with a graceful, flourishing gesture that Mother couldn't possibly be suspicious about. So, boys, feed your lady friends cedar berries. Here's actual proof they are seed for a long successful, happy marriage. The folks celebrated their 53rd wedding anniversary October 28, 1961.

Preface

THIS BOOK IS ABOUT MY PARENTS, and other early-day settlers, and some of the happenings of the early days in the Sandhills of Nebraska.

More happenings have been lost, never to be regained in this great land of ours. Maybe this will help to fill the void.

If it had not been for these people, this great country of ours would have never been what it is today.

They didn't look on any of this as a hardship, but just a way of life and a job to do.

FRANKLIN C. JACKSON

Martin, South Dakota

The Pioneers came in covered wagons
settling in a place of peace and tranquility
called the Sandhills.
It was hard work building homesteads,
fighting off cold bitter winters
Raising families.

Only hard working pioneers
could accomplish this. Families
worked together striving to
keep peace in the beautiful
Sandhills of Nebraska.

By Pat Jackson
(daughter of the author)

Echoes from the Sandhills

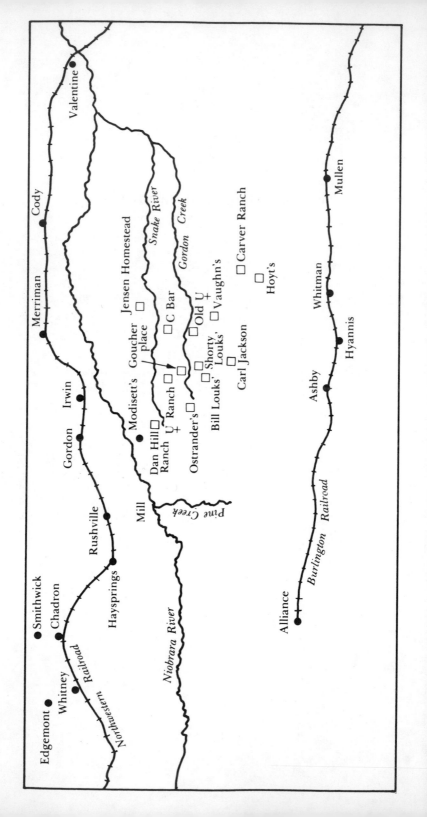

CHAPTER ONE

Coming to the Hills

I HAVE OFTEN THOUGHT that someone should write some of the happenings of the early days.

I often asked my father, Carl F. Jackson, why, when they came to the hills, they came from Smithwick, South Dakota, clear around by Chadron. I wondered if they were afraid of getting lost away from the railroad. There were two brothers, Bill and Shorty Louks, and Dad. They had come to Gordon on the train in the fall of 1911. A man by the name of Bob Boyles ran a cafe where the *Gordon Journal* office is now, and had rooms up overhead. The next morning the two brothers and Dad rented horses and headed into the Sandhills looking for homesteads. Bill located east of the Gourley Ranch on the south side of the valley, Shorty about two miles on east, and Dad in the valley where Roy Dille lived later. My sister and her husband, Wallace Adam, own Dad's homestead now.

They went back to South Dakota, got their stock and wagons and came back to their homesteads. Dad said the reason they came around by the railroad was because it was so wet. If they had come across country, they would still be mired down there.

My oldest sister was the only child my folks had at the time. I have heard them talk about the good times they used to have. When one of them had some special work to do, the others all loaded their families and beds on their wagons and went and stayed until they were done.

I cannot remember Shorty. I met his wife years later when she came back on a visit.

1

Bill was a very good friend of mine. They used to laugh and tell about when they had all gone to a neighbor, by the name of Milo Groves, to put down a well. Of course they had only one-room houses, so when it came bedtime the men went outside while the women would get to bed. This time all the men had gone out but Bill. Finally his wife said, "Well, Bill, aren't you going out so we can go to bed?"

Bill said, "Oh Hell! Go ahead, I am so tired, and my feet hurt so bad I couldn't see anything anyhow."

They were camped on Bordeaux Creek east of Chadron on the way down. The unmarried boys wanted to go to town, so they gave them some money to get some coffee. One fellow was Ben Ekenrod, who later took up a homestead on Gordon Creek. Bill used to tell about how they could hear them coming back, loping their horses and singing. When they came in to camp, Ben had a gallon of whiskey in his arms, but had tied the coffee on behind the saddle. The bag had gotten a hole in it and all the coffee was lost, so Bill said they had to drink whiskey the rest of the way instead of coffee. "Not too bad," he said.

CHAPTER TWO

Putting Up Hay

THE NEXT SUMMER, 1912, they put up the hay on the Carver Ranch. John Bachelor was head of it at that time. Of course they had to have a lot of horses. Bill did the stacking, and Dad and Shorty the mowing.

They had gone to Gordon to get some supplies. Shorty was telling the man that ran the livery barn (the only name I ever heard them call him was Lugen Bill) about their job, and that they were sure going to need some more horses. Lugen Bill said he had about twenty-five head of good horses. Shorty asked if they were broke to drive.

Lugen Bill answered, "Sure, well broke."

They dealt for them, went home with their wagons, and back on a certain day. They met Lugen Bill coming down the Niobrara River road with the horses all strung out. When they got them home, they found none of them was broke. That fall Shorty jumped Bill about it.

He said, "Why, I told you they were broke to drive, and I was driving them when you met me, wasn't I?"

In 1912 when they put up the Carver hay, Dad was twenty-three years old, Bill was five years older, I think, and I do not know how old Shorty was. They had a lot of fun that summer. I have heard them tell how they would get behind all their horses on a rainy day and drive them to Bob Marshall's and trade horses all day. Then they would go home with a new bunch and some money.

CHAPTER THREE

Keeping His Horses

BILLY O'TOOLE told Dad if he needed some more horses that he knew of a fellow who had a bunch to break and, if he took them, to be sure to make a deal where the fellow couldn't take them back until he was done with them.

Dad rode over and made a deal for around twenty-five head of these horse, agreeing that if the fellow took them back before he was done, he was to pay two and a half dollars a head for them. They broke them, which was quite a job as they were all eight or ten years olds.

Right in the middle of haying, this fellow notified

Dad to bring them back. The next Sunday morning he rode over with the horses and put them in the corral, stayed for dinner and after dinner said, "Well, I have to be going so maybe you should pay me for breaking these horses."

He said, "Why, you have mistreated those horses until I don't owe you a thing."

Dad had a palomino horse that he had brought to this country. Floyd Downing told me many times that he was the best horse that ever carried a rope across the Sandhills. Dad walked out, got on him, and as he rode by the gate, hooked his boot toe under the hook of the gate. As it swung open, he let out a holler and took off with the horses.

He said he looked back as he left and saw this fellow run in the house. Dad showed me four or five times where, when he was part way across the valley, the sand started puffing up where the bullets were hitting it.

He made it into the hills. As he went by Bob Marshall's, Bob came out and wanted to know what the trouble was. Dad told him. He told Dad he hadn't heard the last of this yet.

In those days they had a constable and a Justice of the Peace in each precinct. The next day the constable served papers on Dad to appear in court. Dad, Billy O'Toole, Bob Marshall, and Shorty Louks rode over on the day of the trial. The fellow didn't show up, so the Justice of the Peace dismissed the case.

A short time after this, the fellow died. Charley Hoyt and Billy O'Toole used to laugh and say the shock was what killed him, as he was never bested before.

They took the horses on home when they were done haying and used some of them on the freight wagon that fall. Around Thanksgiving Dad got a letter from a lawyer saying that he understood he had a bunch of these horses and, if he was done with them, to please

4

bring them back as they were holding a sale a certain time and would like to sell them.

He took them back as he was glad to get out of pasturing them any longer.

Clint McFarlane, Ben Ekenrod, Carl Jackson, and his palomino horse. Note cowhide laying over fence.

CHAPTER FOUR

Getting Back His Horses

BILLY O'TOOLE lived in Survey Valley. He used to put in a lot of time around Dad's and the Louks brother's camp. Dad said he was a great horseman, and that if he ever saw a horse he never forgot him.

Having so many horses from all over, they were always having some get away. Dad had lost a bay saddle horse that they hadn't been able to find. Along in the fall O'Toole sent Dad word that he wanted to see him.

5

Dad went down and O'Toole asked him if he had ever found this horse. He told him, "No."

O'Toole said, "I seen some fellows across the track west of Mullen with some cattle and one of them was riding this horse. They live south of Mullen."

Dad had a fellow working for him by the name of Stub Ely. Dad told him to get this horse, and not to come back until he had him.

Stub left home one morning and rode to these fellows' place that day; he had an extra horse with him. It would have been around 85 or 90 miles. He had just arrived when these fellows came in. One of them was riding this bay horse. Stub remarked that it was a good looking horse that he rode.

"Yes, we picked him up north of Whitman last summer," he said.

Stub asked if he could stay all night, and kept one of his horses in. That night when he thought every one was asleep he got up, saddled his horse, got the other two, and headed for home. He relayed them all the way home, getting there about eleven o'clock the next morning. Dad told Bob Marshall about it, and Bob asked Stub if he was scared.

He said, "Boy, was I! I was between the devil and the deep blue sea. I knew if those fellows caught me they would hang me, and Carl would have killed me if I had come back without the horse."

I was in the hospital a few years back. A fellow was in my room from North Platte. I was telling him this story. The next day his dad came in, and he told me to tell him that story. I did and he laughed and said, "Boy! Stub was sure right. Those fellows sure had a reputation." He told me their names, but I do not remember them. They were three brothers.

6

CHAPTER FIVE

The 1913 Blizzard and
Another Jackson Came to the Hills

AFTER DAD had done his feeding and turned his cattle in to clean up some stack butts, he left for Gordon with a freight wagon. He got as far as the Dan Hill Ranch the night before the 1913 blizzard hit.

As soon as the storm broke, he took one of his work horses, which he rode bareback, and headed back home. It was around twenty miles.

When he got home, Mother was out pulling cattle out of snowdrifts. She told me many times that she had often wondered afterwards about what would have happened to my older sister if something had happened to her, as she had had to leave her in the house alone. They lost half of the cattle they owned in the blizzard, but they didn't give up.

That summer was very dry in South Dakota. My

Frank Jackson, the morning he left South Dakota, 1913.

7

grandfather, Frank Jackson, decided to move to the Sandhills.

Dad traded for a relinquishment on a section of land that joined him, and went to Hot Springs, South Dakota, to help his father move down. It was around 120 miles. Dad took two horses and rode it in less than two days.

The state of South Dakota had the itch in their cattle so they dipped these cattle—around 250 or 300 head—by hand with coal oil, and headed for Nebraska.

When cattle have the itch real bad, they lose all their hair and are covered with a scab. Under this scab is a mite-like insect you can only see with a microscope.

They had got along fine until they were crossing the Dan Hill Ranch. The foreman came along and was going to turn them back, but they told him it would be closer to the other side of the ranch than to go back, so he let them go ahead.

When they got home, Grandfather went back to get his family.

In about two days there came a government inspector to check the cattle, as the Hill's foreman had reported about them crossing the state line with itchy cattle.

Dad took him over to look at them and told him they had dipped them. This inspector picked out one two-year-old steer that had lost most of his hair, and wanted to know if there was some way of getting him where they could check for these itch mites. Dad said he could rope him. The inspector looked at his horse which wasn't very big and said, "On that horse! I don't think so."

Dad said he took down his rope. He didn't know much about the itch and thought if he washed this steer off real good, maybe, if he had any bugs on him, he could wash them off. He worked him down along the lake, roped him, and upset him into the lake.

He was having a lot of trouble trying to pull him

8

out—more than necessary—kept turning him over. The inspector was running around saying, "Get him out of that water. Get him out of there."

He finally got him out. The inspector scraped off some of the scab, put it under the microscope, said there were no bugs, and declared them clean.

Dad said he guessed "all the bath" he gave the steer wasn't necessary.

CHAPTER SIX

Riding to Town to Dentist and Roping a Coyote

THOSE OLD TIMERS were pretty tough. One time Dad had a very bad tooth. He thought it should come out so he saddled his palomino horse and headed for Gordon, which was 42 miles away.

He rode into Gordon around 11:00 o'clock and went to the dentist who said he would have to cut it out.

In those days they didn't have much to deaden pain so he filled a water glass with whiskey and told Dad to drink that.

He took the tooth out and told Dad to go to the hotel, get a room, and go to bed as that was really going to hurt when the whiskey wore off.

Dad walked out, decided he felt good enough to go home, went to the livery barn, got his horse, and rode home. He got home around 6:00 o'clock. He said the last ten miles he didn't know if he would make it or not as he really got sick.

One day he was riding the little bald-faced horse that he roped the steer off of, when he saw a coyote. He took down his rope and took after him. This little horse was really fast. He ran right up on the coyote. Dad was just ready to make his throw when the horse put both front feet in a badger hole, turned clear over and broke his neck.

It knocked Dad out. A neighbor saw it happen. He hooked up his team to a wagon, got another neighbor to help, and they hauled him home. He didn't come to for about 24 hours, but he didn't go to a doctor; he was kind of under the weather a few days, and had a very sore head.

CHAPTER SEVEN

Buying More Land

PEOPLE COULD DO BUSINESS in those days a lot different than they do now. Bill Louks proved up on his homestead and wanted to sell it as he was dealing on another piece of land right east of Fawn Lake Ranch. It is still known as the Louks' meadow.

Dad told him he would buy him out, but to hold the check until he could get to town. The next day he saddled up and rode to Gordon. He went into the Gordon State Bank to see about getting the money. Iry Magowan was cashier at the bank. When he saw Dad come in, he walked over and opened a drawer, pulled out this check and handed it to Dad saying, "Carl, I don't think this is any good." Boy! Dad said you could have knocked him over with a feather.

Iry laughed and said that Bill was in and said he had to go as some of his folks were sick, and he would like to complete his deal before he left. Iry told him it would be alright as he would take care of it. It was a check for $1500. I don't think these banks could do that nowadays.

There was a fellow lived in the west of what is known as L Lake, now, by the name of Del Hibry. He came up

10

and told Dad the fellow who lived east of him by the name of Steve wanted to see him. He was a bachelor and pretty old. He had taken quite a liking to Dad.

When Dad rode down, he told him he wanted to go to Gordon where he could get on a train to go back east where he had some relatives living, as his health was failing. Dad went home, got his buggy, and took him to Gordon. On the way to Gordon he told Dad he wanted to sell out to him. Dad told him he didn't have the money.

The old fellow said, "Who said any thing about money. We will make up a contract for $1500 for my section of land, and my cattle, 1 team and wagon."

When they got to Gordon, Dad went to a phone and called out to the Fawn Lake Ranch. A new manager by the name of Billy McLaughlin had just come. Dad had not met him yet. He told him about the land, and Mac said, "Well, if it is such a good deal, why the hell don't you buy it?" Dad said it made him kind of mad, as he thought he was doing them a favor, and said, "I just think I will," and hung up.

William McLaughlin, vice president and general manager of Fawn Lake Ranch Co., Lund, Nebraska.

11

He bought it and had it about a year or so when some good friends by the name of Harry and Ruth Henderson came down to see them, driving a new Ford car.

After they left, Dad told Mother he thought he would sell this Steve place for enough profit to buy him a car. He went over and priced it to Mac. Mac bought it and they went to Gordon and made the deal. When they were done Mac said it would have been a lot cheaper to have bought it when Dad called him before. Dad said, "Well, I told you it was a good deal."

He and Mac got to be very good friends after this.

CHAPTER EIGHT

Being a Midwife

MRS. DUNCANSON was known as a midwife to many people. As it was a long way to town she was called on many times. Her husband had been a doctor. One time when my father was away, Mother had gone to stay with her; it was really snowing. They were getting ready for bed when a knock came on the door, and there stood a boy. He said his dad had sent him to get Mrs. Duncanson, as his mother was having a baby.

Mother decided to go along. She had to take my oldest sister also as they could not leave her home alone. It was about two and a half miles. The snow was very deep, and it was still snowing.

Mother says she can still remember how the horses would lunge through the drifts as they could not see in the dark to miss them.

They finally made it and were just in time to help with the baby.

About 50 years later some people came to the folks' place and introduced themselves to the folks. They said their folks had homesteaded in the Sandhills. Their names were Roteman. They stayed for dinner, and Mother was telling them about this incident. The man grinned and said, "Yes, I am the boy that drove the team and I can still remember how it was snowing. Mrs. Duncanson was an aunt of my wife."

A few years back a lawyer called Mother and wanted her to come down to his office to sign some papers. Here it was a paper to identify a girl who was trying to get a social security number. Her folks had said that Mother was midwife at her birth. She had been. The folks were coming home from a dance, when this fellow came out and stopped them, and said his wife needed help.

As a funny coincidence this was the place where Mrs. Duncanson had lived at one time.

Jennie Duncanson, Catherine Jackson holding Franklin, Charlie King, Jr., Carl Jackson, and Gladys in front.

13

CHAPTER NINE

Buying a Mean Bull

DAD WAS IN GORDON with a freight outfit one time. He was hooking up at Lugen Bill's livery barn the next morning when a fellow came in and wanted to know when Bill would be shipping some cattle as he was going to have to get rid of his bull before he hurt someone.

In those days they didn't have sale barns. When someone had a few head of cattle to ship or sell, he had to put them in with someone else's.

Dad asked this fellow what kind of a bull he was and he told him he was a Hereford.

Lugen Bill spoke up and told Dad he was really a good bull, but he was surely mean.

Dad asked the fellow what he wanted for him since he sounded like just what he needed, as he was having a lot of trouble with the settlers north of him going through his pasture and leaving the gates open. He said he would take a hundred dollars for him.

They agreed on a date and Dad went back and got him.

He put him in his pasture and put signs on all the gates—*A Mean Bull in Pasture. Beware of Him.*

A Jew by the name of Rosenbaum lived north of Dad. (The Fawn Lake Ranch has the land now, but it still goes by the name, Rosenbaum.) He was one of the worst about leaving the gates open.

About a month after Dad got the bull, Rosenbaum was going through. The bull saw him and took after him. He was in a wagon. The bull upset the wagon and Rosenbaum had to spend the night under the wagon because the bull wouldn't let him out. When the bull upset the wagon, he broke the tongue out and the team ran away.

14

The bull finally left for water the next day. Rosenbaum crawled out and went home. He always went around after that, and Dad didn't have any more trouble with his gates.

About a year after this Dad went down to get his bull to take him home. He was in a pasture east of home with some cows. Dad was coming up along a lake with him, when his horse stepped into a rat run and fell down. The bull turned around to take Dad. The lake was frozen over. Dad crawled out on the ice as his horse had jerked away when he saw the bull coming.

It was about a quarter of a mile up the lake to where a fence crossed the lake. The bull followed out on the land all of the way trying to get out on the ice to get at Dad, but every time he would slip on the ice and have to go back to land. Dad had to walk about two miles home.

Dad had a neighbor by the name of Cy Porter, and he had trouble with people leaving gates open, too. Porter wanted to buy this bull.

Dad took him over there one day. Tom Stewart and Fred King, my wife's uncle, were there. They ate dinner. Porter thought while he had so much help there he would just brand the bull.

Dad got on his horse. Someone opened the gate. He rode in and roped the bull by the hind legs. He jumped off his horse to help the fellows hold the bull, and the rope broke.

Stewart and Porter made it to the fence, but Dad and Fred couldn't make it so they headed for the barn. Fred was in the lead. As Dad went in, he tried to swing the barn door shut but only got the top one.

The bull was right behind them. Dad jumped and grabbed the rafters. He looked around to see where Fred was. He was in the manger.

They used to put boards up and down in the mangers

15

so the horses couldn't knock the hay out. These boards were always about six inches apart.

As Fred was a short, real heavy-set fellow they never could figure out how he made it.

My brother-in-law was talking a year or so ago about coming in from out at the corral with my Dad one day. Wallace had a narrow place he always went through. He told Dad he thought they had better go around as Dad probably couldn't get through there. Dad told Wallace he could go anywhere he could, that he had proof a heavy-set man could get through a real narrow place, especially if a bull was after him.

In those days when it came time to prove up on their land, they had to go to Valentine, Nebraska, which is clear to the other end of Cherry County, about 90 miles, so they would go to Merriman to take the train to Valentine. It would have been around 50 miles from Rosenbaum's place to Merriman.

Harry and Ruth Henderson, taken in the 1960s.

16

Harry Henderson was telling me one time about how Rosenbaum had walked to Merriman and taken the train to Valentine. When he got back to Merriman, he went to a saloon and bought a gallon of whiskey—to have a celebration when he got home.

Harry didn't know whether he had been sampling the jug or not, but he was about two miles from home when he slipped and broke the jug on the frozen ground.

I'll bet the air was pretty blue there for a while!

CHAPTER TEN

Freighting and Trouble

DAD ALWAYS KEPT four head of horses up, and grained them whether he was working them or not. He had four head—one strawberry roan, a blue roan, and two brown horses. They were all half-brothers. He freighted with these horses all the time. He would freight for other people and for himself. The blue roan horse was the one he rode home after the 1913 blizzard.

He made a trip to Ashby. He used to carry a bed roll and camp outfit most of the time. On the way to town he left some hay and his stuff in an old sod house on the south side of a lake. I think they call it the school section. The land belongs to the Castles now.

When he got to Ashby he stopped at the lumber yard—it was where Bill Crouse's garage is now—and went on to the livery barn to put up his horses. These weren't very large horses, but real good workers.

There was a fellow at the barn buying artillery horses for the British army. He said, "If those horse weigh 1400 pounds, I could give a good price for them."

Dad said, "Well, they are not for sale, but that blue horse will beat 1400."

17

The fellow said, "Well, I have five dollars that says he won't."

Dad didn't have but five dollars with him, and though he thought he could go without his dinner, he didn't like to short his horses. But he thought he was safe, so he bet him.

He kept edging toward the stock tank while he was talking; he thought if he could get some water in them he would be sure to win, as he had just driven them forty miles and wasn't sure.

The fellow said, "Here. Here. Don't let those horses drink."

They led the blue horse back to the lumber yard and weighed him. He weighed 1430 pounds. The fellow paid him, and Dad took the horse back to the livery barn, and went to eat his dinner.

When he came out, here was this fellow leading the blue horse back to the barn. Dad hollered, "Here, what the hell are you doing with my horse?"

The fellow laughed and said, "Here," and handed Dad two dollars. He said, "I had to protect myself and bet a fellow who just came to town that the blue horse would weigh 1430 pounds and, of course, he did." He said the two dollars were for the use of his horse.

Dad loaded up. The weather looked real bad, and the man who ran the lumber yard, by the name of Joe Maupin, wanted Dad to stay in town. He told Dad he might not make it somewhere before the storm hit.

Dad didn't tell him he had a place to stay, but left town. It was around eight miles to where he had left his stuff. When he got there, it was really snowing. There were two rooms in the sod house. He put his horses in one room and he took the other.

When he awoke the next morning, there was a blizzard on. He stayed inside all day and the next night. He said he was very comfortable as the horses kept the house warm,

18

and he had plenty to eat. The only thing that bothered him was that his horses had no water. The next morning the storm had broke so he headed on home.

I think this was the time that one brown horse was sick, so before Dad left home he got a gray mare in to make the trip with. She hadn't been worked since haying the summer before, and with the snow so deep, the horses would have quite a time going through the drifts. She would get to fighting and get a leg over the tug, and would she kick!

When Dad got home, he was pretty near wore out, and just dropped into bed and went right to sleep.

Mother used to laugh and tell about how in the night, she must have bumped against him or something. Anyhow he grabbed her leg and said, "Damn you. I am getting tired of you kicking something all the time. I will just break your leg." She said she thought he would before she could get him awake.

He always looked cheap and said he thought it was the gray mare kicking him.

CHAPTER ELEVEN

Freighting and Too Many Dogs

DAD FREIGHTED all over the Sandhills. He used to say that he wished he knew how many miles he had hauled capstans and cable for the Bell Ditching Company.

They ditched all over the country with this outfit. He hauled it from the Jensen Ranch that the Minors have now to the Clayball Ranch that the Fairheads own now north of Merriman. That was the last time he hauled it. When they were done there, they shipped it by railroad to Rushville and hauled it out to Pine Creek and ditched it. They left their equipment there and quit. I helped use one of these capstans twenty some years later to move a house on a foundation at Hank Beguin's.

I have heard my brother-in-law tell about how, when they ditched there at Jensen's, they would have this capstan set up on a hill with the cable running out into the valley, as much as one-fourth of a mile away, to the ditcher.

He says he has seen this cable break, and as soon as the horses would hear it, they would drop clear down as this cable would snap back and could kill them very easily. They would work sixteen head of horses on these capstans. They were a round drum-like concern and, as the horses walked around and around, the cable was wrapped around the drum and pulled the ditcher out in the valley.

Dad used to tell about when he had gone to Hyannis one time for a load for someone. He had put his horses in the barn on the north side of the tracks, when the manager of the livery barn came in with a bottle of Hokey Pokey acussing; he bet he would put a stop to all the damn dogs sleeping in his barn. There was a dog or two asleep in each manger, and, of course, the horses couldn't eat the hay.

Dad said he went down each stall and would pour a little on each dog. As he poured it on the last dog, the first ones were starting to take off. When he came to the last stall, there was a milk cow in there, and Dad said he guessed he didn't want to waste any so he just poured what he had left on her.

Dad said they stepped into the barn door to watch the dogs. They were really taking off. You could hear them all over town, really howling. He said there was one going right up Main Street.

There was a lady crossing the street. Someone hollered, "Mad Dog!" She really took off for the grocery store; the dog saw her and was going right with her. When she came to the door, the dog did too. She just stood there and screamed as she couldn't open the door with the dog in the road.

Dad said they really had a lot of noise because about that time the poor old cow went to bucking and bawling in the other end of the barn. People couldn't figure out what all the excitement was. He said you could see people come out of their houses all over town trying to figure out what the noise was about. They surely had a good laugh.

When I was a kid, I can remember Dad wouldn't get done haying until pretty close to the first of October. Then he would put two freight wagons on the road until the weather really got cold. The first two wagons hauled a load of coal, a ton of flour, two hundred pounds of sugar, and other groceries. I can remember that if the winter was real bad, people used to come to borrow flour and sugar, as they knew they always had plenty on hand.

Dad always fed cake to his cattle and raised quite a few hogs, so it meant a lot of trips to town. It took three days to make a trip.

I can remember one time Dad and Frank Hamilton sold their pigs to someone at Rushville, which was fifty or sixty miles away. They must have had around three hundred head of these pigs and they trailed them all the way to town. Dad had taken our dog, the one that Gladys and I had saved from the Indians. The dog had eaten some coyote poison somewhere, so they had to feed him all the cooking lard to save him. When they got to town, they were going down the street when a car went down the street and the old dog took after it. He always chased cars. They couldn't get him to come back. Dad surely hated to come home and tell me he had lost my dog.

About six weeks later, Nelly and I went to school and here was our dog. Frank Hamilton had found him over at the Post Office. He had a bad scar where it looked like someone had shot him.

21

A year or so later at a Fourth of July celebration, Mother was visiting with two old maids who lived about half way between our place and Rushville. They were telling about how a yellow dog had come to their place one night. He had been shot and was almost dead. They took care of him, and he stayed with them about a month and then left. They didn't see him again. We felt sure that this was our dog, and surely felt thankful that they had taken such good care of him.

My grandfather had given me this dog when I was about two years old. I can always remember that when I was going to get a spanking from Mother, if I could just get outside, he would not let her up to me. I really thought he was a great dog.

CHAPTER TWELVE

Easy Money

THE COUNTY ON EAST of Survey was settled by a colony of Jews. When they proved up, they sold out and left the country. Horses were cheap, and they had a lot of young horses, so they just left them.

When the war broke out, there was a demand for horses, so these Jews sent a young fellow out to see if he could gather these horses. He came to Hyannis and someone told him he could probably get Dad to gather them.

He rented a team and buggy from the livery barn and came out. He hired Dad to gather the horses and take them to Hyannis for fifty dollars.

Now, there were two fellows by the name of Bob Wolfe and Tom Stewart who had leased a place from a fellow by the name of Harms. There was a lot of farm land on this place and they had to have a lot of horses, so they had

22

gathered these horses and broke them to work. Dad and Tom Stewart were very good friends so Dad knew they had broke these horses.

He rounded up the horses and took them to Hyannis. When he got there this Jew met him at the stockyards. As far as the man knew, these horses were unbroke.

He said, "Boy, Mr. Yackson, I sure woosh these horses were tied up. I have a buyer who would pay a good price if they were."

Dad said, "Well, you get me some halters and rope. Bring them down here. Then get away as I can't have anyone around watching me when I am handling horses. I will be done in about an hour."

The Jew did this. They had agreed on two dollars a head for the job. Dad had the horses all tied up when he came back. He was surely well pleased and gave Dad his one hundred dollars. There were twenty-five head of these horses.

Dad got on his horse and headed home. I think he stayed at Rolfe Brenneman's that night. He had borrowed a horse there when he came by as his horse got sick. I have heard him tell about what a good horse it was.

The next day he met Charley Hoyt who was really riding a good bald-faced bay horse. Dad asked him what he would take for him. He said, "$100."

Dad said, "Well, if you will give me a halter to lead him home, I will take him."

Charley told him that any time he could sell a horse for $100, he would give a man a halter and his dinner, so they rode on over to the ranch and ate.

Now, Dad knew there was a horse inspection in Gordon the next day, so he went home, stayed all night, and went to Gordon the next day. The horse passed inspection and Dad got $150 for him.

He used to laugh and say that was the easiest money he ever made. He only had to ride 150 miles, and he liked to ride anyway.

CHAPTER THIRTEEN

More About Horses

DAD USED TO BUY and trade a lot of horses. He used to get them from all over. He got a brown horse that had come out of South Dakota.

Horses have a habit of trying to go back to their old homes, especially in the spring of the year. This brown horse had come up missing. Dad had asked around in the north country about him.

One day when he was in Gordon, Orville O'Conner, the father of the one on the Saults Ranch now, came to him and asked if he was short a brown horse. He said this horse was up on the Overton. This was a ranch owned by the Spade, and he was boss there. (It is now known as the Hull Ranch, and belongs to the Minors.) He said if Dad would come up, he would help him get the horse, so Dad rode up there one day.

A boy by the name of Walt Lefler was working there. They had a little trouble at noon so O'Conner fired him.

After dinner Dad and Orville went after this horse. When they came back into the valley at the ranch where they were haying, Orville looked at the fellow raking hay and said, "Why, that is that Lefler kid." He loped up and hollered, "I fired you at noon. When I fire a man, I want him to stay fired."

This kid says, "Oh, Hell, if a man paid any attention to you, he would be looking for a job all the time. Gedop!" and he went on raking hay. He worked there for several years after this.

The Jensens came to the Sandhills of Nebraska before the turn of the century, in the fall, from around Edgemont, South Dakota. They settled south of Merriman. They rode after their stock all that winter, and the next spring, as soon as the ground thawed out, they went to building fence.

24

Julius Jensen was one of the boys. His oldest son afterwards married my oldest sister, Gladys.

Julius said after about three days he went to look at their stock, and they were short three head of saddle horses. He started out to hunt them. He rode to the Modisett Ranch—about 30 or 35 miles and stayed all night. They told him the horses had been there a day or so before. The next morning he rode on up to the mouth of Pine Creek where a fellow had a flour mill.

He told Julius the horses were there the night before, that he had better put his horse in and eat dinner. Julius said, "No," if he was that close to them he would get right after them. He rode up the creek about ten miles, and finally lost any sign of them.

Pine Creek is the only creek I know of in the Sandhills that part of the time flows west.

He headed on west. The next day at noon he caught up with the horses around twenty miles north of Whitney, Nebraska, aloping right on north. These horses had made a trip of around 140 or 150 miles trying to go home.

Julius said he took them down and sold them to Tom Stansby on the JL, the next spring, as he didn't want to make that trip again. He said they were just building the old ranch house there at that time.

CHAPTER FOURTEEN

Buying a New Car

WHEN DAD GOT READY to buy his new car, he and a neighbor named Claude Grover (later Dad bought him out) rode to Gordon horseback.

Dad bought a new Chevrolet. They got a neighbor by the name of Harry Hebbert, who was in town with a freight wagon, to lead their horses home as far as his place.

They had a little trouble getting home as there weren't many roads in those days—just trails and wagon roads. Then, too, neither of them had ever driven a car before.

It was quite an occasion when anyone got a new car in those days. Several of the neighbors would go to town to help. When another neighbor, Lee King, decided to get a car, why, there were four of them who went to get it.

He bought a Model T Ford. I have heard them tell about how much trouble they had. He had never driven a car either.

He was always getting in trouble and killing the engine. They would have to get out and crank it. One fellow bought a sack of grain and put it in the back seat. Dad thought it was a good thing he was behind Lee as he even threw the sack out once driving so fast around a bend in the trail.

They got to Dad's late that night. Everyone was real tired and went right to bed after they had eaten. Ben Ekenrod used to say Lee got out of bed in the night and tried to crank his bed in his sleep.

Lee King became my father-in-law as I married his oldest daughter, Elsie Lee.

CHAPTER FIFTEEN

Getting a Ranch, More Cows, and a Son

DAD SOLD THE HOMESTEAD and Bill Louks' place and dealt for a place from Walter Goucher.

Walter Goucher had married his oldest sister, but they didn't live together very long.

Dad went to Gordon and bought a bunch of cows, mostly shorthorn. I can remember some of these cows. He added more land to this Goucher place and had a pretty good ranch. It was a little strung out, but he operated it for 30 years before he sold it to Henry Ahren.

Dad bought out some fellows by the names of Clint McFarlane, Roy Hibry, and Claude Grover. Afterwards he bought out his dad and his oldest sister which was our summer range. It was about six miles from our home place.

From what I understand, the winter of 1916 and 1917 was a pretty hard winter. As the folks lived so far from town, they decided Mother should go to town ahead of time, and so she went in February. She said that was the longest time she ever put in in her life. I was born the fourteenth of March, a day after my Dad's birthday.

I have heard Dad tell that he was feeding and he could see a fellow coming from the north, following the ridges. In about half an hour he rode up. It was Milo Groves. He was working at the U-Cross at the time. Whenever there were any messages, they would call the Ranch by telephone, and they would bring the message over. It was six miles straight south from the Ranch to our place.

He said Milo rode up and said, "It's a boy, Carl."

In a few days Dad and my oldest sister went up to see us. Dad said it was a long trip in a buggy for a little seven-year-old girl, so he had to figure out some way to entertain her. It was a warm day; the snow was really melting and there was water running in all the draws. He thought they could think up names for the streams which, he said, worked good going to town, but when they came home the water had all dried up and she seemed to think he should be able to remember all the names. She had stayed with Dad alone and gone to school.

Just think what a job that was to get a little girl up and ready for school every morning. She had about a mile to ride horseback.

27

Dad had around 300 cattle to care for at that time. Although he had an Irish man working for him I don't know as I ever knew his name—only "Irish."

CHAPTER SIXTEEN

Shipping from Ashby at Flu Time

DAD, WALTER GOUCHER, TOM STEWART, and Joe Duncanson shipped out of Ashby. It was late in the fall. There was an outfit moving from the Carver Ranch to south of Ashby as near as Dad could remember. As near as I can remember the name was Fickeron.

They had been laid up in Ashby for several days. The men were all sick with the flu. Dad said two of the men died the day they loaded their cattle out.

They had beds in the church for the sick, and the rest of the fellows were rolling out their beds in the school house at night.

When they got loaded out, Dad said, "Let's go home." The other fellows wanted to stay in town as it was cold, and snowing pretty hard. He and Joe Duncanson had their beds together. Joe didn't want to go home, but Dad left and told him he guessed he would have to come if he wanted to sleep in a bed.

They rode to the valley north and east of Sterns. There was a sod house, so they put their horses in the stack yard and rolled out their bed in the house. Carrying a bed on a horse makes it always warm from the horse's body heat, so they had a nice warm bed.

Dad said Joe surely crabbed about riding into the storm all the way from Ashby. It was around 18 or 20 miles, I think.

The other fellows all got the flu. It was a month before Walter Goucher got home. Tom Stewart died, so Dad said Joe used to claim he thought Dad saved his life.

CHAPTER SEVENTEEN

Hail Storm and Loose Horses

I WAS IN HYANNIS to a rodeo last fall and met a man by the name of George Jones. I hadn't seen him for a number of years.

He was telling me about how the country had changed up north as they had driven out to Dad's old place and stayed all night the night before.

He had worked for my Dad a number of years in haying. He went on telling about one time when they had 14 head of horses running loose over in Fawn Lake Meadow, with the harness still on, in a hail storm.

Dad had told me about this many times, and had shown me a rake wheel that was bent in the middle where the team had run into a stack of hay with it.

George said when the storm came up, Dad hollered to every one to get their horses unhooked. There was a kid running a rake. He evidently was excited and didn't get one tug unhooked when he dropped the neck yoke. The team took off and, of course, this one tug being hooked, they took the rake with them and tore it all to pieces.

George said he could still remember how cold it was out there catching their horses after it quit hailing, as no one had any coats, and the ground, he said, was just as white as though it had snowed.

They went right through a high range of hills north of Dad's house to this meadow. They used a buggy. One day a wheel broke on this buggy, and they left it. It was in an out of the way place. I rode this pasture for several years when I was a kid and had never seen it.

This was a rough range of hills and was our horse pasture as well as where we kept our milk cows. I would have trouble finding the cows or some horses and would go home and say I had looked everywhere and could not find them.

Dad would say, "Well, did you find the old buggy?"

I would answer, "No."

He would say, "Well, you haven't rode the whole pasture yet." I would have to go back.

I can remember yet the day I found it. I was around seven or eight years old. Dad had got Roy Dille to come up to stack hay that afternoon. He told me to get a certain team. I rode and rode and couldn't find them.

I came up on a hill and here in a pocket in the hills was the old buggy. I just turned around and loped my horse all the way home.

I rode up and said, "I can't find Dick and Jasper, and I rode the whole pasture because I found the buggy."

I still had to go back and hunt for the horses as he knew they were in there. I found them, but still didn't think it was fair because I had found the buggy and knew I had "rode the whole pasture."

CHAPTER EIGHTEEN

Getting More Cattle and the Blizzard of 1920

DAD AND TOM STANSBY went to Wyoming the fall of 1919 and bought steers. Dad never did tell me how many Tom bought, but Dad bought 600 head.

He said every night when they were going to bed, Tom would remark about how the paper would read the next fall, that "Tom Stansby was in with some choice two-year-old steers, and Carl Jackson was in with some feeders."

Dad said Tom would buy the top end, and he would buy what was left. He called the U-Cross to send word over home that he would be in Ashby a certain time and for Irish to bring down a string of saddle horses and a camp outfit.

Dad got into Ashby in the night, unloaded his cattle, opened the gate, and let them out. He thought they would eat along the right of way, as they were really dry in Wyoming, and these cattle had not had much to eat. They had been on the train for over 24 hours.

The next morning he got up real early, told Irish to get breakfast and he would get the steers. He took down the track toward Hyannis. About six miles east of Ashby he met a man driving the cattle.

He said, "These your cattle?"

When Dad told him, "Yes," he said he had picked up the leaders right in the edge of Hyannis, which is nine miles east of Ashby.

This fellow's name was Chris Abbott. This was the first time Dad had ever met him. Afterwards they got to be good friends.

When they got about four or five miles out of Ashby, there was A. R. Modisett in a car along the road. He asked Dad what he would take for the steers. Dad told him they were not for sale. When he came down the hill at Sterns, about 15 miles, there he was again. He said he would sure like to buy the steers. Dad still said, "No." He asked Dad what the steers cost him. Dad told him.

When he came through the Jones' pass about three miles from home, there he was again, horseback. He told Dad if he wanted to take the steers on to the Ranch, there was $5000 profit in it for him. Dad said he thought if he could pay that, when he already had them, they should make money, so he said, "No."

He said many times, "If I would of just took it . . . ."

Dad wintered these steers. McLaughlin told him he ought to take them over and put them in the C-Bar Meadow, as that was where they were putting theirs. As they were to summer together they just as well get used to each other. Dad was getting short of feed. Since they wanted to clean up the meadow, Dad decided to do this.

The day before the 1920 blizzard, Irish and Dad took these steers down there, around 15 miles. Dad has told me

31

many times about how, when they were coming home, they talked about what a beautiful evening it was. The next morning the blizzard was on.

The day the blizzard was over, when Dad came in to dinner, Mac was there. He asked Mac how things were.

Mac said, "Not too good." All he had found so far was one horse and he was dead.

Mac said he had followed the steers into the valley north of Dad's which is known as Fawn Lake. He guessed the steers were trying to come home, but had missed the turn at the east end of the lake, and had gone on west. After dinner they saddled up and went after them. Where they crossed the Gordon Creek, the banks of the creek were pretty deep. Mac says, "Well, this is where we will find a lot of them when the snow comes off."

Jess Trueblood had a lot of cattle at the Ostrander places, as he had bought their hay. This is where Cal Westover is now.

His cattle had joined them there. About a mile later they found their first dead steer. It was a Trueblood steer. After that they would find one every once in a while.

They found the cattle in the high hills north of Hebberts. Dad said you could pretty near have made a 90% cut on those cattle. The Trueblood cattle were first, and had come the least distance. The U-Cross cattle were next, and the Jackson cattle were in the lead. These steers of Dad's had not had any feed but cotton cake all winter. He and the U-Cross didn't lose any cattle. Trueblood had lost a lot of cattle.

The U-Cross cattle and Dad's cattle had drifted a good 25 or 30 miles in the storm.

I have heard the Hebberts tell about, when they got up the morning after the storm, their hills were just black with cattle. There were around 2500 or 3000 cattle in the bunch.

That fall the price of cattle really dropped. Dad went to town and went to the bank. He said he was going to ship. He was banking with the Gordon State Bank. Hill told him he was foolish to ship these steers. They were holding all of theirs, and thought that was what Dad should do.

He has told me about how the U-Cross was shipping wherever they could get cars. They were to ship out of Ashby that week. He was running the U-Cross wagon, so, instead of taking any of his cattle, he just took more U-Cross cattle. They were loading out when Logan Musser came. He was the president of the U-Cross, and wanted to know where Dad's cattle were. He said they were home on the range.

The black saddle horse, Johnny, Dean Jensen, Jerry Jackson, and Dwight Jensen.

He said Logan really ate him up. They went to Omaha. The only decent word Logan said all the time was when they went into a cafe to eat supper one night. He told them to bring the biggest T-bone steaks they had as Dad still had a lot of cattle on the range, and they had to keep the price up somehow.

When Dad got home, he and Mother talked it over. Dad knew the U-Cross was shipping everything they could, so

33

he and Mother went over and got all the odd colored and poor end of the steers and shipped them.

The next year he shipped the rest, and just had enough money to pay the bank. He had lost his two years of feed and his labor. If he had not shipped what he did the year before, he would have gone broke.

He didn't have much faith in bankers' advice after that.

CHAPTER NINETEEN

Horses and Roping a Coyote

BILL LOCY RAN A STORE and post office at Allen, South Dakota. He did a lot of trading with the Indians and got a lot of horses.

Mac bought 100 head from him. Among them was a black horse. Dad used to tell about him, and what a good horse he was. I cannot remember this horse, but I can remember some of the others.

While visiting with my cousin the other day, he told about my Mother and older sister going back to visit her folks in 1916. This must have happened then, as I don't remember my folks ever going anywhere alone without each other.

The U-Cross boys and Dad went to a place south of Survey known as the Martindale Post Office for the Fourth of July celebration. They rode horseback and it was around 25 or 30 miles. Dad rode this black horse. He roped a coyote on the way down and won the horse race and calf roping on him after he got there.

I have had a lot of arguments with fellows nowadays about the horses now and then. They talk about how much better the horses are now. I would like to see one of their horses now do something like that, as they have to

34

haul them in their horse trailers even if they're only going a few miles to work.

Harry Henderson says the Janice and Pouriers raised more good race horses accidently than most fellows who were in the business. He says he knew one horse the Janice's had. He was a brown horse; he has known them to ride this horse 100 miles to a celebration and win everything on him after they got there.

Catherine Jackson and Gladys Jackson.

CHAPTER TWENTY

Buying Hay and Moving Cattle

DAD WAS HELPING at the Ranch. It must have been in about 1918. It was a real bad winter, and they were getting real short of hay.

One morning at the breakfast table, Mac told Dad to go down to Vaughn's, which was around fifteen miles, and buy his hay. He said, "Buy it as cheap as you can, but buy it."

The snow as really deep. It took him all day to ride down there. He said that he and Vaughn sat up until around twelve or one o'clock in the morning visiting and dealing on the hay.

The next day they measured the hay—around 1000 ton. Dad stayed all night again, and went back to the Ranch.

Coming up the valley to the Ranch you can see for a mile or so. Dad said he could see Mac walk out to the barn and back two or three times as he was coming up the valley.

As soon as he rode up, Mac said, "Well, did you get it?"

Dad said, "That's what you sent me for, isn't it? But I don't know how you are going to get any cattle there as it takes a good day to make the trip horseback in the snow."

He said Mac spun around and headed back to the house, and said, "Why the hell don't you let me worry about that?"

The next morning he told Dad to take one man and go out on the summer range and gather what horses he could and come east to meet them. Dad said when they got to the Dutch Henry gate with around sixty horses, the rest of the men were there with around a thousand cattle. Mac waved them on ahead with the horses to break trail. Horses can go through snow where cattle can't.

They got to Vaughn's around one or two o'clock. Mac rode over and turned these horses through the gate into the meadow. He and Dad would run them around each of the stacks two or three times, as the snow was really deep around the stacks.

They stayed all night and the next morning, Dad said, the snow was frozen around the stacks until they could drive around them anywhere with their feed sled.

They took their sixty horses and headed back to the Ranch. They made it in about three hours. I have known other times when horses were used in this way. Those old fellows didn't have tractors and bulldozers; they did with what they had.

The barn at the U-Cross burned down a few years ago. They were trying to figure out when it had been built. I asked Mother, and she said she couldn't remember. The first time she was at the Ranch was in 1913. She couldn't remember if the barn was there at that time or not, but she hardly thought so as the ranch house was just a shack at that time.

She said she could remember that they used to tell the story about when they were going to paint it once. Musser wanted to paint it white. Tully wanted to paint it gray.

Mac had stood there and listened to their argument, turned around, started for the house, and says, "I don't give a damn what color you paint it, just so it is red." So it was painted red.

She didn't know if this was when they first built it or not, but thought it was.

CHAPTER TWENTY-ONE

Striking Oil and About Some Friends

BILL MCLAUGHLIN was a wonderful man. He was a man of great honor and integrity. He was a plunger in business and made and lost several fortunes in his lifetime.

He and three or four other fellows invested in a wild-cat oil well in Wyoming. Dr. Copsy of Alliance was one of the men. I never knew the others, and have forgotten their names.

They struck oil, and called Mac to tell him, and asked for him to come out. He came over and wanted Dad to go with him. Dad didn't think he should, but Mother wanted him to go. So Mac sent a fellow over from the Ranch to stay at Mother's and do the work.

Dad and Mac took the train from Gordon to Wyoming. When they arrived at the closest town to the well, they hired transportation out. They had quite a time finding any way, as the road was full of transportation. Some people were even walking. Dad used to tell about this as the only boom he was ever in. He said he remembered the older fellows telling about the gold strike in the Black Hills, and wondered if this was the same.

When they got out to the location, there were around 500 people there already. Someone had set up a place to serve meals. I don't remember what the price was, but Dad used to tell how expensive it was.

It was raining and had been raining for some time. He said the place was churned up into about six inches of pure mud.

One fellow had put up a tent, and had several bed rolls rolled out in it. He was charging $5.00 for six hours in a bed. There were lines waiting to get in. They only stayed around 24 hours and came home.

A. J. Vaughn, the man Dad bought the hay from, was another character. He came out from Missouri and started up a store in the Hills. I understand he had a doctor's degree, but he never practiced in the Hills.

He was an investor in land. He owned one large ranch, and had investments in land all over when he got killed in about 1935 or 1936. A horse ran over him and killed him.

He was a great one to walk wherever he wanted to go. He would walk up to Dad's, about 10 or 12 miles, to catch a ride to town on a freight wagon. He used to laugh and tell me how Dad's place had the shortest nights of any place he ever stayed. He said Dad used to take him out to the bunk house to sleep. In those days all the lights they had were coal oil lamps. When Dad came to call him, he would burn his hand on the lamp chimney as it had not had time to cool off yet.

He used to walk up to the Ranch and have some big deal on. He would tell Mac about it. If Mac thought it was alright, they would take Mac's car and go to town. Sometimes they would be gone several days.

38

Dad said Mrs Mac would see them coming and would say, "Well, the big boys had a successful trip," or "They never got along so good."

Dad would go out. If they had had a good trip, they would come in and eat, and Mac would have Dad take Vaughn on home, but if their trip hadn't been a success, Vaughn would get out and take down the road afoot. Mac would always wait until he was out of sight. Then he would tell Dad to go and take the old so-and-so on home. It was around 15 miles.

Dad asked Mrs. Mac how she could tell. She said, "Oh, that is easy. If they are both in the front seat, they have had a good trip. If Mac is driving and Vaughn is in the back seat, they haven't got along so good."

One stormy day, Dad, Mac, and Vaughn were out in the bunk house visiting. Mac tipped back on the back legs of his chair, listening to Vaughn telling a story, when his chair collapsed with him.

Vaughn looked over at him and said, "Boy, I have spread a lot of it in my time, but that is the first time I ever had a fellow swallow so much of it, he broke his chair down." Dad said Mac sure got up and stomped off to the house.

Another good friend of theirs by the name of John Mulligan used to tell the story about coming home from town after a hard rain. He and Mac were in the front seat and Vaughn was in the back. They came up over this hill. The road was washed out. The car shot out on high center and came to an abrupt stop. Vaughn came clear up into the front seat.

He looked up at Mac and said, "Boy, Mac, that was quite a bump."

Mac looked down at him, saying, "Well, we sure didn't need you to come up here and tell us about it."

CHAPTER TWENTY-TWO

Moving Houses and a New Baby

IN 1921 DAD MOVED the buildings from his dad's homestead to the Goucher place. He had to go through four ranges of hills and across the Gordon Creek with them.

He had a hired man, and he would have to get up early to get breakfast, put up a dinner, then drive down there, six miles, to work, in a wagon or a buggy.

My Mother was in Gordon. Dad kept my sister and me at home with him. He would have to take us down there with him. I can remember how long those days were.

Dad's car wasn't working anymore, so when my youngest sister was born, we had a long trip to go see her.

Dad hired a man to bring Mother and our new sister home in a car when they were ready to come. His name was Dennis Gardner.

They had to jack these houses up, put logs under them, and chain them to wagon wheels. They used 16 head of horses to pull them. He got Roy Dille to put his horses on and help.

They just got them moved, but didn't do any more to them until the next year. They sure looked forward to getting them fixed up as they only had a two room house and three kids now.

My sister was born the fourth of June. You used to always start haying right after the Fourth of July. Mother had a big hay crew to cook for. I never knew her to have a hired girl.

CHAPTER TWENTY-THREE

Gathering Steers

ALL THOSE OLD TIMERS life was cattle and horses.

I have had several different fellows come up to me, shake hands, and say, "Boy, I knew your Dad. He was surely a wonderful cow man and a top cowboy."

I couldn't help but think—a few years ago I saw Felix Becker. He was telling me about going to Europe to see his daughter, and how many countries he was in. He told me, "Never saw a damn thing," because he hadn't seen any cattle. That would have been my Dad all over.

Dad and Mother, in later years, traveled a lot. Dad would come back telling about the cattle and horses he had seen, and how they cared for them in different places.

When they used to run big steers, some of them used to get located with someone's cows and were pretty hard to get. Dad used to put in about ten days every fall at the Star Ranch gathering these steers for them. I have heard him tell about a steer one time at the Johnson place, about eight miles west of the Star.

Dad came up by Hooper's and stopped to visit awhile. Hooper said, "You just as well go on back, Carl, and save your time and horse, as the only way you will ever get that steer is with a wagon." That was before trucks.

Dad rode on up. Johnson had just turned his milk cows out. This steer was with them. When he saw Dad he turned around the end of the lake. Dad headed right across the lake.

I say there aren't many fellows left that have swum any more water than I have horseback, because Grandfather and Dad always went straight for where they were going. If there happened to be a lake in the road, they just went across. Of course, I rode with them both many miles when I was a kid.

The steer saw Dad coming. He said he guessed he

41

couldn't figure out what that fellow was going to do because he just stopped and watched Dad cross the lake.

When Dad got across, he took down his rope and caught the steer by the hind legs, got off and tied him with his piggen string. He took his knife and slit the steer's nostril, put his rope through it, tied the other end to his saddle horn, and let him up.

He said for a while he thought he was going to tear the rope out, but the nostril is a very tender place. They sometimes put a ring through here to handle bulls.

When he went by Hooper's, he said he could just swing his rope and turn the steer any place. Hooper surely laughed. He told Dad he was the fourth man he knew of that had tried to get this steer.

Lee McDonnell was another good cowboy. He used to go up every fall and gather the Modisett steers.

One fall a horse fell with him and broke his leg, so Lee could not go.

Modisett came down and asked Dad if he would gather them for him. The Modisetts were out of Texas, but came there from Virginia. They had a lot of funny ideas, as far as the people here felt.

Dad went up. Modisett told Dad there was a steer up at Wuthier's, and to go get him. It was only eight or ten miles. Dad rode up there and got the steer. He got back to the Ranch about ten o'clock, and put the steer in the corral.

Rosa Coddier came out. Dad had put his horse in the barn and was sitting by the side of the barn in the sun. She said, "Mr. Jackson, did you get the steer?"

Dad said, "Yes, he is in the corral."

She said, "Well, A. R. is not going to like this. When he tells a man to do a job, he expects him to take the day to do it." She was Modisett's sister.

The only time I was ever around the Modisett Ranch was when Dad sold them his steers in the fall of 1931. He made arrangements to deliver them on the weekend so I could help him. We had made arrangements to stay at a fellow's place that night, but it was early in the day, so Dad told me to ride over and tell the people we would not stay. We went on to the Ranch.

When we were right southeast of the Ranch, here came a horsebacker out. It was Mr. Modisett. He was riding the chore boy's horse. The chore boy was a real short fellow, and Modisett was real tall, so his legs stuck away up over the saddle. He came riding up and said, "Mr. Jackson, I don't know where we are going to put these cattle. You weren't supposed to be here until tomorrow." There were over 30,000 acres in the Ranch.

Dad says, "Oh, I guess we can find some place."

We left the cattle and rode on up to the barn. Modisett said, "Well, you can see if you can find a place to put your horses in there. I don't know if you can or not, as you weren't supposed to be here until tomorrow." We put our horses in.

The foreman came out and said, "I guess you can come on up to the house, Carl, and I will let you sleep in the extra bed in my room. A. R. doesn't know where to put you, as you weren't supposed to get here until tomorrow."

We went to the house. They had a large room with a lot of easy chairs and books in there. It was called the "Cowboy's Lounging Room."

The Hebberts and a fellow by the name of Glen Hoselton were there with their cattle.

After the rest of them went in to supper, Modisett came to the door and said, "You fellows can come on in. I guess there are places for you to sit, even if you weren't supposed to be here until tomorrow."

After supper he would come and call some fellow's name, and he would go in and get settled up. The last fellow in was Roy Hebbert. When he came out, he looked up at the clock and said, "Well, Carl, you can go in, in 15 minutes.

43

A. R. will try to settle up with you, although you weren't supposed to be paid until tomorrow night."

That was the only ranch I know of, in the West, that had individual salt and pepper shakers, just like in a restaurant. The meal was served individually, just like a restaurant. We had a very small steak, a few vegetables, and a slice of bread for supper. For breakfast we had one egg, one piece of toast, one piece of bacon, and four corn flakes.

When we left after breakfast, I was complaining about the meals. Dad laughed and said, "Well, I had grapefruit with my breakfast."

I said, "Yes, I noticed it." The foreman always bought his own grapefruit, and when he went to eat it, every time he stuck his spoon in, some of it would squirt into Dad's face.

We had a lot of fun about this in later years.

CHAPTER TWENTY-FOUR

Running a Hay Crew and Getting to Ride in a White Car

MAC HAD A LOT OF FAITH in Dad. One fall he was having a lot of trouble getting his hay up. There was a fellow by the name of Tully running the crew. He was not having very good luck with the men. Mac told him to go over and tell Carl he needed him.

Tully says, "Why, he can't come as he doesn't have his hay up yet."

Mac says, "You tell him I need him. He will come."

Tully came over and told Dad he was supposed to report to Mac.

This may be the time Tully gave us a ride in his car. My oldest sister was asking me a few years ago who it was who

44

gave us a ride in a white car. A few days later it caught fire and burned up. How glad we were that we got to ride in it before it burned! I could not remember, but when I asked Mother she said it was Tully.

Anyway Dad went over, and, in the process of getting the crew straightened out, he fired one fellow who was a good friend of Mac's. This fellow smarted off to Dad, and bet he wouldn't be fired long.

A day or two later Dad rode up to the Ranch. Here this fellow was, mowing the lawn. Dad walked in the office and said, "Figure up my time, Mac, I am done."

Mac says, "What is the trouble, Carl?"

Dad told him, "You know damn well what the trouble is, When I am running an outfit and fire a man, I expect him to stay fired. Not have someone go over my head and hire him back."

Mac says, "Well, all right. I will send him to town on the wagon in the morning, Carl, but you sure are a hard man."

U-Cross hay camp.

45

CHAPTER TWENTY-FIVE

Roping a Dog and a Steer

MAC WAS ALWAYS taking Dad somewhere to do some work, so he was not surprised one day, when he came riding in for dinner, to find Mac waiting for him.

Mac said, "Put your saddle in the car, Carl."

Mac always drove a Hudson car and, if the weather was nice, he always had the top down.

After dinner they left for town. Mac had a brown or bay horse that was really a good horse. He kept him up town during shipping season. I think his name was Buttons. When they got to town, he told Dad to saddle this horse and go help them in the stockyards with the cattle. Dad thought it was funny that he brought him clear to town to help them, as there were two fellows with the cattle.

He saddled up. As he was leaving, Mac says, "Oh, Carl, there is a steer out there with the town herd. Just as well pick him up as you come by."

In those days a lot of people in town kept a milk cow, and they would pasture them together.

Well, when they came by, Dad picked up this steer and put him in with the other cattle. One of the fellows laughed and said, "You will never make it to the yards with him."

When they got pretty close to the yards, the steer broke back, and Dad took after him. Just as the steer went over the grade Dad roped him. As the steer went over one side of the grade, the horse was starting up the other side. The rope came tight and the horse missed his footing and fell. He was on one side of the road and the steer on the other. They were both down. Neither one could get up as the rope was too tight.

The fellows put the other cattle in the yards and came back to help. They put their ropes on the steer and pulled him enough to get him up, then took him to the yards.

46

Mac says, "Well, I told you all it would take was a cowboy to show you fellows how to get that steer."

They had got him that far four other times. He would always head back and get away.

One other time Mac told Dad to get his rope and come with him. When they got across the Niobrara River, he said, "You tie that rope to something, and when we go by this place up here, rope that dog when he comes out."

Dad did. He said Mac really speeded up. The rope didn't come off until they were a couple of miles up the road. The dog was dead.

Mac says, "Well, I bet he doesn't chase any more cars, or bark at any more cattle when they go by."

CHAPTER TWENTY-SIX

Putting Up Hay on the Old U-Cross

MAC WAS LEAVING the Ranch in the fall of 1922 and did not care about expense. He wanted Dad to put up the hay on the Old U-Cross.

Dad told him he couldn't put it up, as he had no car. He couldn't get to town to get help. It was around fifty miles to town. Mac told him if he would take the job, he would bring him the men and pay him a good price.

It's funny how a person can remember, after fifty-four years, moving down there. It was around ten miles. They used three wagons to haul furniture, beds, and groceries.

Each wagon had four horses on it. One wagon hauled the chickens. Mother had hatched out over 300 chickens under setting hens that spring. They had to take them for meat as they had no deep freezers or refrigerators in those days.

My oldest sister and I drove the milk cows. Boy, did we

47

think we were big! They drove the rest of the horses ahead of us. Around sixty or seventy head of them.

It was around the first of July and it got pretty hot. A lot of the chickens smothered and died. I can remember how bad Mother felt.

I can remember what a time they had with help as it was right after World War I. The fellows were real unsettled. I have often wondered about how the folks ever got done. It rained all summer, and the men were coming and going. It must have been pretty discouraging.

Haying on the Old U-Cross.

I can remember one time when there were twelve men for supper. The next morning only two were at the break-fast table.

My sister's and my greatest enjoyment was going up in the hay mow of the barn and watching Dad rope the horses for the men in the morning and at noon. The corral was west of the barn. It still was the last time I was

Haying on the Old U-Cross.

there. We could open the west door and sit there with our feet hanging over the edge.

Dad used to tell about seeing Julius Jensen some place. He asked him how he was getting along haying. Julius said he was going to have to buy some tents to keep his harness in to keep the moss from growing on it; it was so wet.

Everyone used to laugh about having three crews that summer, one coming, one in the fields, and one going to town.

One time Dad and I were out by some mowers when Mac drove up with a load of men.

He says, "Carl, can't you be more easy on these men? I have a hay crew of my own to keep going."

They had some little caps with just straps over the top, and a celluloid brim. That was the style at that time and most of these fellows were wearing them. Dad said, "Well, if you would bring me someone without one of those go to hell caps, and without his sleeves rolled up to his elbows, maybe I could keep them."

Just then a fellow rode up. He didn't even have a hat on,

Haying on the Old U-Cross. These pictures reproduced by courtesy of Bert Schrader.

and his sleeves were cut off at the elbows. He had just got out of the army, and come to Whitman. Someone told him that Dad was out there haying. He rented a horse at the livery barn and came out. He had worked for Dad before and Dad knew he was a good hand. He said, "How about a job, Carl?"

Dad said, "You bet, Bill. Put your horse in and get ready for dinner."

Mac just put his car in gear and took off. The wheels threw sand all over Dad and me. As he left he hollered, "Why the hell don't you practice what you preach?"

Mac hadn't known that Dad knew this fellow. His name was Bill Kirby. He worked for Dad several years after this.

My sister had made a hammock out in the trees. Mother didn't have any help but my oldest sister. She didn't have time to take care of my baby sister, so we kids had to take care of her. We had taken her out one evening and swung her in the hammock until she went to sleep. All of a

50

sudden we heard Mother scream. She could always do a good job of that.

We ran to see what the trouble was. She had gone out to shut up her chickens and had just shut the door when a mother skunk and nine little ones came out of a hole in the ground right beside her. She thought it was some kind of a black and white snake. She grabbed us kids and got us in the house. These skunks were running all over the yard. Mother wanted to know where her baby was. We told her she was asleep out in the hammock. Then she was afraid a skunk was going to find her and eat her up.

We had quite a time convincing her that she would be all right where she was. When the skunks left we went out and got her.

One evening a big Indian came to the door. He asked Mother if this was Carl Jackson's hay camp. Mother told him it was.

He said his name was Tom Spotted Bear and that they would camp right out there. He pointed right outside the yard.

My sister and I had always heard about how Indians eat dog. We had a big yellow bob-tailed shepherd dog. We caught him and took him out to the barn. We sure worked hard leading him upstairs in the hay mow, as we didn't want them to eat him.

When Dad came in from work he sent them up the valley about a half mile to a flowing well to camp. I can remember how Dad took us kids out to hear them singing and dancing that night.

You could sure hear their drums. They were heading for North Platte to join a Wild West show. There were around fifteen or twenty wagonloads of them.

The next morning they came down trading horses with Dad as it had rained and they could not hay that morning.

51

CHAPTER TWENTY-SEVEN

Losing Their Horses

DAD USED TO TELL about one time when Mac and Vaughn had been gone. They got back just as a bad storm hit. Cattle all over the country were mixed up. They had been working them three or four days. When they got Vaughn's out, he said if they would loan him a horse, he would take them home. The U-Cross had a sorrel horse that Dad said he had never liked. He told Vaughn he could just have him and to keep him.

Dad had had a horse that got hurt at the Ranch, so Mac gave him a real nice four-year-old brown horse. These horses both had the U-Cross brand on them and, as Mac was leaving, Tully thought he was going to be in line for the job. He wanted to show authority, so he gathered up all the U-Cross horses and took this one of Vaughn's and Dad's.

Dad just had this brown horse started good when Tully got him. He told some fellows he would just keep him for his own use.

Tully saddled him up and the horse bucked him off. He never could ride him; Tully had really spoiled him. I can remember they had this horse at the Ranch for years and about all he ever did was buck.

Anyway, when we were down on the Old U-Cross, here came Vaughn; he was really mad. He said they took his horse, and he wanted Dad to go get him back. Dad told him, "Hell, Vaughn, I can't get him back. They took mine too."

Vaughn didn't like it but thought if Dad had lost his horse, why, it would be all right, although Dad had given him this sorrel horse.

CHAPTER TWENTY-EIGHT

Starting School
and Building a School House

IT WAS REMARKABLE how much work those old timers could get done, and nothing ever seemed to daunt them.

When the folks finally got done at the U-Cross that fall, they had to get home and put up their own hay yet. They had around 800 tons to put up, as Dad always put up one meadow north of his place for the U-Cross for years.

They didn't get back home until around the first of September that fall. They had put up around 2500 tons at the U-Cross. It was a lot different than it is now as this was all with horses.

The east end of the barn at the Old U-Cross.

My sister and I started to school right away in a sod school house. There were the two of us and two Dille children.

As soon as Dad got done haying, they went to freighting lumber for a new school house.

Dad, Bill Kirby, Roy Dille, and a carpenter by the name

of Swan Swanson built the school house. They built it between the Dille place and us. We each had about two and a half miles to go to school.

Eight of us children started and graduated from the eighth grade from this school. My oldest sister, of course, graduated here, too, but she didn't start at this school house. She didn't go through all her grade years in the country, as they didn't have school in this district for several years.

After they got the school house built, they went to work fixing up the house that Dad had moved off of his father's homestead. We sure thought we had it made as we had a four-room house then.

Dad moved one room of the old house at the Goucher place to our new location, for a bunk house.

CHAPTER TWENTY-NINE

School, Teachers, and the Old Sod School House

SCHOOL WAS ALWAYS HARD for me. I have often wondered if it was on account of not going to school but five months the first year, as the teacher quit, and six months the next year as I was sick. I always passed, but if it hadn't been for my Mother, I know I never would have.

The first teacher got married after school started and her husband came to stay at our place, too.

He had a car, and Dad had given him a job trapping. Dad would always carry Mother's supply of water for the day before he left. This fellow would wait until time to go to school, then he would take two buckets of this water and fill his car. He would take the teacher to school and let my sister and me take her horse to school, so she would have a ride home.

Mother had told Dad of this. So one morning Dad did as always and left. Right after he left this fellow got his water and started out to put it in his car.

He always drove his car right up to the door of the house. Just as he came out of the house, Dad stepped around the corner. I can see this yet. Dad grabbed one bucket of water and turned it right upside down on his head, kicked him at the same time, and grabbed the other bucket before it could spill and threw it on him.

"Now," he said, "get up that hill, get your own water, and fill them buckets, and put them back where you found them."

They had to carry this water down a hill as Dad had put a well on the hill, so we could have running water in the house. He hadn't got the pipe in before the ground froze up that fall.

This fellow sure went up the hill, got the water, changed his clothes, and took the teacher to school.

Us kids all thought it was pretty good as they sat out in the car all day until the middle of the afternoon. Then the teacher handed in her resignation and they both left.

My sister Gladys was in the seventh grade, so the folks made arrangements for her to go to another school for the rest of the year. None of the rest of us went any more that year.

When Gladys started to school in the old sod school house, there was a fellow by the name of Speck who taught the school.

I have heard her tell many times how there was a big bull snake which stayed in the walls of this school house. He would come out when the school house would warm up. Speck wouldn't let them do anything to him. He said he was very harmless and killed mice and rats. When they tore down this school house, they found a big bull snake over six feet long. I wondered if it was the same one. They weren't as thoughtful as Speck; they killed it.

55

CHAPTER THIRTY

Losing a Friend and Making More

MAC LEFT THE RANCH in the fall of '22. I can remember how Dad hated to see him go. He said he had sure lost a good friend and neighbor, that he would never have another that good. But he was mistaken. The Rosseters were the new men. Clyde was the general manager and Mose was the foreman.

Dad started them both in at the Ranch that winter. I have heard Dad say many times that he never worked with a young fellow as nice as Mose was. He was only 21 at this time. He and Mose became very close friends.

I can remember how Mose used to come over for years and ask Dad for advice. He stayed a lot of nights at our place.

I can remember that a few years back I met Milford Johnson in Gordon and was visiting with him about the Ranch.

He says, "Do you know what that Mose had me doing this summer?"

Mif had worked for the Ranch for twenty years or so and had even run a hay crew for them for several years.

I said, "No. What was that, Mif?"

He said, "He had me down on the Old U-Cross raking hay for Albert Hebbert."

"Well, that was about right," I said. "Dad always said a man ought to sweep hay for fifteen years before he knew how to rake hay."

Mif says, "Huh! Well, that is another of those ideas that Mose got from Carl then."

One time Dad and I met Chris Abbott and stopped to pass the time of day.

After we went on I remarked that there was a man the Abbott Corporation would surely have a hard time replacing.

Dad said, "Yes, but no man is indispensable. But I can

56

tell you a man that they will have more trouble replacing than him." I asked him who that was and he said, "Mose Rosseter."

I asked him how he figured that. He said, "Well, Abbott has all those banks and ranches. He has a man on each one; he could just drive in and tell them what to do. But Mose does it all: the bossing and the financing both."

I can remember when Mose died and Johnny Kime took over. "Why," I remarked, "that is a good job for Johnny." And Dad said, "Yes, and Johnny is a good man for the job, as he has lived right beside the Ranch all his life. He knows how it has been operated and it will just go on like it always has."

Mose ran the Ranch for 41 years. He was a great horseman. I don't think there was a horse on that ranch he couldn't just look at and tell you his mother and age. I am sure they ran as high as 600 or 700 horses at one time.

Mose Rosseter on his top horse, Possum.

CHAPTER THIRTY-ONE

Getting Another New Car and Two Disappointments

IN SEPTEMBER OF 1923 Dad got another new car—a Ford touring car.

His horse corral was about a mile from school. The next morning he took my sister and me to the corral and let us walk on to school. He told us if we would hurry home from school, he would quit early and take us to the post office after school.

We had told the Dille children about our new car, and that we would be by after school so they could see it.

I can see Dad yet, coming up the valley with his mower as we came through the hills. Boy! We sure ran to be there in time when he was ready to go.

We got in the car. He cranked it up and away we went. We had to go through a very bad range of hills north of Dille's. We could not make it and had to go back to take the men home. I can remember how disappointed I was because we didn't get to go by Dille's so they could see our new car.

The other time was a year or so later. My sister had come home for Christmas vacation. When Dad took her back the weather really looked bad.

He met a man by the name of John Van Ausdale, horseback, about ten miles from town. Dad told him to just tie his horse up and go back to town with him, so he would not be afoot if the weather got so he could not make it.

John did. When they got to town, Dad was hurrying around getting his supplies and met another neighbor by the name of Ed Ostrander. He asked Dad if he was going home. Dad said, "You bet."

Well, he would just go, too, then. He had taken his daughters back to school also.

They left town. It was snowing hard when they got to where John had left his horse. He went on ahead to show them where to go.

After about six or seven miles they got stuck. John went on to the Hill Ranch. A fellow by the name of Felix Nern had it leased then. He got a sled and team, then came back and got them. They made it about ten miles farther to the Enlow place. A fellow lived there by the name of Heywood. Dad borrowed a horse and rode on home—about ten or twelve miles farther. Ostrander stayed at Heywood's.

Of course Dad had to leave all his supplies in the car.

It was around the first of April before the snow went off enough that he thought he could make it home with the car. He and the hired man rode up there horseback. The man led Dad's horse back while Dad brought the car home.

I knew they had gone that day so I really loped my horse all the way home from school. I knew Dad had bought some oranges when he had gone to town and I could just taste them all that day. Mother came rushing out to see why I was riding so fast. I told her that I hurried home so I could eat some of those oranges.

She said, "Why Franklin, Dad threw those oranges away. They had frozen and were spoiled." Boy, was I disappointed as we didn't have much fruit in those days.

CHAPTER THIRTY-TWO

Reading by Candle Light

I DON'T KNOW WHY my sister, Gladys, had a vacation the winter that Dad had left the car, but she had come out to the U-Cross Ranch and came on over home horseback.

The snow was so bad that we hadn't had any mail for

about a month. Gladys rode over to the post office the next day and got the mail.

We were out of coal oil for our lamp since Dad had taken the barrel to town to get some and it was in the car yet. Mother had made us some tallow candles. That was all the light we had.

At this time there was a paper printed in Omaha called the *Omaha Daily Bee*. My folks had a subscription to it. When my sister got home, she had a big sack full of mail. I can see Dad, Mother, us three children, and the hired man sitting around the table that night reading the papers, and the folks reading their letters.

That would be some experience for people nowadays, but we thought we were really living it up.

I can't remember how my sister got back to school in Gordon, but she probably rode back to the Ranch and went up with someone from there.

Indian camp at Gordon Fair. © Miller.

CHAPTER THIRTY-THREE

Working Overtime

DAD USED TO LAUGH about how Logan Musser never wanted to lose any time on Mose or him.

He said they would come riding in some evening and here would be Logan's car in front of the barn. He would say, "Just put your saddles in here, boys."

They would eat supper and head for the Star Ranch, which was about forty miles away, and all country road.

They always ran steers at the Star at that time—no cows at all. They would trail the steer calves over there in the fall, and run them there until they were three years old. They wintered the bulls over there, too.

They would get over there around eleven or twelve o'clock at night, and be ready to go the next morning. He said in about a week or ten days, when they would be done over there, there would be Logan some night, and they would go back to the U-Cross after supper.

Dad used to tell about one time when they first got over to the Star and had put a bunch of steers at a certain place. A school teacher, who hadn't been able to get a job that year, was to feed them.

They had been there about a week when Mose asked him one night how the steers were doing.

He said, "What steers?"

Mose says, "Why, the steers you are feeding."

He said, "Why, I haven't seen any steers."

The next day Dad and Mose rode down to where he was feeding. Dad said he had never seen so much hay scattered out in his life as there was. The steers were gone. They had found a hole in the fence, and had gone back to where they had been moved from. This fellow had just scattered hay each day for a week.

Dad used to tell about another time they went over to the Star. The next morning, when they were catching

61

their horses, there was a good looking mouse-colored horse in the corral. Dad was looking him over, when Chris Mosler, the boss, came in the corral. Dad asked him about the horse. He said he had been there about a year, and that he belonged to the Greens. Chris didn't think he was broke. Dad said it looked to him like it was time he was, so he caught him, and saddled him up. He said he bucked a little. He rode him most of the time he was there. One day he and Mose rode over to the Green's place. Dad tried to buy him but they wouldn't sell. Dad always wondered if they appreciated getting him broke for nothing.

One time when the snow was really deep, Musser and Tully came out to the Star Ranch with a bob sled. They had come as far as Hooper's and stayed all night.

The next morning when they were leaving, Hooper just grabbed a scoop shovel and said he would go with them, as they might have some trouble.

Dad said Tully used to say he didn't think it was the trouble Hooper was worried about; it was all the whiskey they had along, getting away from him.

When they were going in to dinner, they could see these fellows digging out a gate about one-half mile from the ranch. When they came out, they just drove up, and Musser jumped Chris about not having the gates scooped out.

Chris stuttered some. He said, "Well b-b-by god, if you don't l-l-like to sh-sh-shovel out the gates, you could go around." The fence was torn out on both sides of this gate, but they hadn't torn the gate out because it was a big wooden one.

CHAPTER THIRTY-FOUR

A Fourth of July Celebration

IT WAS BEFORE the Fourth of July in 1923 that Dad and I rode by the old sod school house. The Gourleys were tearing it down to get the flooring for a place to dance on the night of the Fourth. This is when they killed the bull snake.

Dad had given me a white pony that he got when he bought out Clint McFarlane. He was a beautiful animal and weighed about 900 pounds. He never did have a speck of any other color on him even when he died at the age of around 25 or 26 years of age. His mane was so long it almost hung to his knees.

I will always remember the morning of the Fourth. Dad had taken his bath and put on his clean clothes, except for his shirt and overalls. (He put his old ones back on.) He never changed them before he had harnessed up the buggy team.

There was a small lake over in the hills. The horses liked to stand in this when the weather was hot to fight the flies.

This pony had lain down in this lake with my sister and me many times when we would ride out there to get the horses.

Dad always told us that was foolishness and that, if we were riding a horse the way we should, he couldn't lay down with us.

Anyway, here came Dad in with the buggy team. He was wringing wet. The horse had lain down with him in the lake. It was the white horse, as we always kept him in a small pasture for a wrangling horse. We surely wanted to laugh, but we didn't dare.

The reason I can remember this celebration so well is because a fellow by the name of Lawrence Macumber, who had worked for Dad, got bucked off of a Vaughn mare there that day. (As near as I know this mare was never "rode.") This sure tickled me as he had always teased me so bad when he worked for Dad.

Carl Jackson and his "modern conveniences."

CHAPTER THIRTY-FIVE

Radio and Modern Conveniences

DAD WAS A GREAT BELIEVER IN modern conveniences. I think my mother was among the first of the women to have a washing machine. It was quite an affair. It was an old wooden tub contraption run by a gasoline engine.

I wouldn't know how many horse-power the engine was, but it was a massive concern and ran the machine by a long belt. In the summer it ran the sickle grinder with a belt through a hole in the wall of the wash house to the sickle grinder.

Either one would be a collector's item today.

I think it was probably in about '27 when they got a new Maytag washing machine. They really thought they had something then. It ran by a gasoline motor too, but much smaller.

The first radio I can remember belonged to a well driller by the name of Lee Ander Mower, who came to our place to put down some wells for Dad. He had a radio that had ear phones. We would take turns listening on them. I sure thought that was something.

Dad got running water in our house in the spring of 1923. We were about the only ones in our part of the country who had running water in the house at that time.

I think it must have been in about 1926 when Dad got us a radio. It was a Fada radio. An Atwater Kent speaker sat on top of it. It was a huge thing, but my Mother surely enjoyed it. She would sit in front of it in her rocking chair in the evening and listen to it.

It was the ending of a wonderful era in our lives. Dad always trapped in the winter time. He would sit and skin muskrats after supper and Mother would read books to us before we got the radio. We surely enjoyed the books. It seemed to make for closeness. Dad trapped the U-Cross for years.

CHAPTER THIRTY-SIX

Letting the Other Fellow Gather the Horses

I ALWAYS THOUGHT it was marvelous how those old fellows knew what was going on, and how they got things done.

65

When I moved up south of Rushville, I got acquainted with a fellow by the name of John Dykes. He was one of the best storytellers I ever knew. I have always thought it was such a shame someone didn't get some of the history of the Hills written down that he used to tell about.

He was telling a story about when he lived on a place that belonged to Fred Beguin, the same house I helped move with the capstans years later.

He was just eating breakfast one morning when a neighbor by the name of Wuthier came in. He talked very broken. He said, "Shawn, I no can find my horses. I look two days, can't find hide nor hair of them. You find them. I give you twenty dollars to get them."

After breakfast John said he saddled up, rode over east about twenty-eight miles, and stayed for dinner. After dinner he went out, untied his horse, and started to get on, and said, "Oh, say, Wuthier is pretty upset about his horses. He is going to Valentine on the train in the morning to report to the sheriff." He got on his horse and rode home.

He said he was eating breakfast the next morning when here came Wuthier. He came in and said, "Shawn, that was fast work. I get up this morning. Here is my horses in the corral, and here is your twenty dollars." John used to tell this and laugh about how he didn't even have to drive the horses to get them home.

CHAPTER THIRTY-SEVEN

A Trip to See the Grandparents

JUST BEFORE THANKSGIVING in the fall of 1923, my mother's sister, who lived near Hot Springs, came to Gordon on the train. Dad went up and got her.

A few days before Thanksgiving, we got up real early,

ate breakfast, and left for South Dakota, to visit the grandparents. Their names were Mahoney.

We went to Merriman, Nebraska, across country most of the way. There were no roads. Mother had put up a lunch for us, but we didn't stop until we got to Winner, South Dakota, after dark that night. We stayed there all night; it was about 150 miles from home.

We drove all day the next day, crossed the Missouri River at Chamberlain, on a ferry, and drove up to Grandfather Mahoney's about supper time. He lived near Fulton, South Dakota.

I will always remember how Dad drove up and sent Gladys in to see if we could stay all night. Now the people in the east are funny about things like this. Gladys went up and knocked on the door. Grandfather came to the door. Gladys asked if we could stay all night. Of course he hadn't seen her for about seven years, so didn't know her.

He said, "Oh, we never keep people all night. It is eight miles to the next town. You can stay there."

Gladys says, "Oh, I think we will just stay here. That is what my dad figures on doing."

The old gentleman just came a stomping out to the car to tell Dad they couldn't stay.

When he got out there, there sat the folks, laughing at him. He looked pretty cheap. Of course we stayed all night.

I have heard my mother say that he used to always keep a stallion. He would drive him around the country on a cart to breed mares. He had bred a mare for one man who would not pay him. One day Grandpa saw him in Fulton, South Dakota. He asked him for his money. The fellow said he did not have it. Grandfather walked back to his buggy, got his whip, walked up, and said, "You better get the money," and hit him with the whip. The fellow took off, Grandfather after him, right up Main Street. Everyone came out to see the excitement, and the fellow paid up.

The Grandparents, James and Anna Connell Mahoney.

CHAPTER THIRTY-EIGHT

Getting a New Saddle and the First Trip to the Railroad to Ship

THE SUMMER OF 1924 Dad went to town one day. He told me he might bring me a new saddle.

I remember that from noon on, I very nearly wore the path out to the front gate, looking for him to come.

When he did come, I could hardly wait until the car stopped till I was on the running board. Sure enough there was a new saddle in the back seat. I sure crawled right in and got it. There was even a new rope tied on it.

They don't make saddles like this one any more. Even most of the big saddles are not this good.

I rode it until I outgrew it. I don't know how many calves I roped from it.

One winter I even pulled the teacher's car to start it, until the folks found out and put a stop to it.

I still have the saddle. My younger sister, my younger brother, and all five of my children have used it until they outgrew it. The tree is just as good as it ever was.

The next day after Dad got the saddle, we left for Ashby with some cattle to ship.

It was 40 miles. Dad used to always laugh and say he didn't want either the Northwestern or the Burlington railroad to think he showed any preference; our spread was halfway between them.

Dad had told me that since it was so nice and warm we would just sleep in a hay stack.

I had never been over this trail before. We left our cattle about dark. He said we would ride up the valley a ways. We could probably find a stack to sleep in.

We had gone from our place to the pasture where the cattle were and cut out the ones we wanted. We had ridden about 20 miles and I was tired. Well, we came to a gate. Dad got off to open it. I rode through and there was a haystack just a little ways. I rode over there, got off, took my hobbles off my saddle, and started to put them on my horse. I heard Dad holler, "Franklin."

I said, "I am right over here."

Dad rode up and says, "What are you doing?"

"I am getting ready for bed," I answered.

"Oh, let's ride on over here a ways. I think there might be a better place."

"Oh, I am tired," I said. "This one looks good enough for me."

"That looks like it might have a lot of stickers in it. Come on, let's go a ways farther."

He had to really put up a talk to get me back on my horse. We rode through some hills and there was a house where Tony Senn and his wife lived. We stayed there that night and I was always good friends with them after this.

69

The next day we ate dinner at John Barnes' place and stayed that night with some people by the name of Gillus. They weren't on our road, but Dad had known them in South Dakota when he was a kid.

I can remember Mrs. Gillus' father lived with them; he was blind. I don't think it was very nice the way I watched him, but it fascinated me to see a blind man. He was real old or seemed so to me. The next day Dad told me he had lost his eyesight in a mine explosion in the Black Hills, when Dad was just a kid.

We got into Ashby early the next day and crossed the railroad west of town. The stockyards were east of town at that time.

There was no fence south of where the highway is now, and we were letting our cattle fill up there when we saw another bunch of cattle come through north of town with just two riders. They seemed to be having trouble getting them across the tracks. Dad said we would go help them.

We rode up there and I was running my horse to head these cattle, when all of a sudden he really jumped and almost lost me.

After we got the cattle across the track, this man said, "Come here, young fellow."

We rode back to where my horse had jumped. There was a big rattle snake. He killed it and gave the rattles to me. There were ten of them. That was the biggest rattle snake I think I have ever seen and I kept those rattles for years, but they finally got lost in the shuffle some place.

The people with the cattle were Clyde and Mamie Thurston.

Dad and I went up on the hillside where our cattle were, got off our horses, and lay on the ground to rest.

Clyde came up and said, "Carl, this land belongs to a fellow by the name of Charlie Mauch. He is pretty tough about fellows stopping here."

70

Dad said, "Oh, I am not scared of him."

Clyde had not much more than left when a fellow came over the hill as hard as his horse could run, waving a whip, and hollering, "Get those cattle off of there."

Boy, I got right up and on my horse. I was not taking any chances.

Dad just lay there. This fellow came right up to him. When he was close enough to see Dad, he said, "Why, hello, Carl! Boy, your cattle sure look nice."

Come to find out, Dad had found a two-year-old steer of his clear up on the U-Cross a year or two before, and had sent word to him. Charlie had come up to get the steer, got caught in a snow storm, and had to stay a week with the folks. Of course Dad didn't charge him for that, so I guess he thought he owed Dad a little grass.

Clyde asked Dad what he had on that fellow as no one else could stop out there.

Dad laughed and said, "Oh, it is my good looks."

After we loaded the cattle out, we started home. Got out of town about four miles when Dad remembered he had forgot to send a bill of sale for a McFarlane cow, so we rode back to town, and put our horses in the livery barn. Dad mailed his bill of sale.

We went on up to Shelly Fields. Dad got us a room. I wanted to go home, but Dad thought it would be too far, as it was late at night by then.

Mrs. Fields was freezing some ice cream. Dad bought me a big dish so I thought it would be alright to stay all night. We went home the next day.

I forgot to tell about the second day when we came through the valley south of the JL. We saw a badger which Dad roped for me. I drug him along on the end of my rope through the hills until we came to a flowing well tank on the Sterns' land.

Dad took the badger and drowned him in the tank. All

cowboys have a dread of badgers on account of the holes they dig. A horse can sure fall when he steps in one.

Dad told me to drag him away up on the hill where no one would see him as Mr. Sterns would sure be mad if he knew Dad had drowned a badger in his tank.

When we got to Sterns, he was out working in his garden. Dad stopped to visit with him.

I took the cattle and went right on. When Dad caught up, he wanted to know what my hurry was. I told him I didn't want to have anything to do with that man.

I never did tell Mr. Sterns about this. He would have really got a kick out of it.

I have stayed at the Sterns' many times. They are really swell Western people.

CHAPTER THIRTY-NINE

Going to Visit Mac and More About Horses

WHEN MAC LEFT the U-Cross, he went up and bought a ranch on Bear Creek, northeast of Martin, South Dakota, from Spurgeon Waddill.

Dad thought we should go up and visit them after he finished haying in the fall of 1924.

There was a boy from Martin who had worked for Dad that summer by the name of Louis Babby. He had come down horseback and sold his horse to the U-Cross that fall. He rode back home with us.

There still were not many roads in the Hills. Dad always went about like he rode—straight as he could go.

Years later I was in Lessert's hardware store in Merriman. A fellow by the name of Louis Mason asked me how far it was from Minors' north place across to the Card place. I told him it was about 30 miles by the road. He said, "Oh, it can't be."

Louis Babby was working there at the time. He came out from under a car and said, "Say, Louie, I don't believe I would argue with him about the Sandhills. I don't think there are probably any two fellows know those hills any better than him and his dad. The first time I ever crossed the Snake River in a car was with his dad. We just came straight across the hills and forded the Snake River. I don't think many fellows would attempt that now, even with their four-wheel drives. All he had was a Model T."

Mac was a very great man. I don't know of any other man that seemed to have their hands on the pulse of the country like Mac did. A man here at Martin told me about how hard Mac worked to get the Bennett County High School made a county high school. That is just the kind of man Mac was. He had no children in school any more, and never would have, but he was still interested in the school.

When Otho Kime was sheriff of Cherry County, I helped him take a man to the asylum at Norfolk. I said something about Mac.

"Oh, do you know Bill Mac?" he said. "He is sure a great man. If I need to know anything about anything, if I can just get up to Mac, he can give me all the answers."

We spent a couple of days at Mac's and headed back home.

We came through Martin. Of course, being a kid, I am probably mistaken, but it didn't seem like there was much to Martin, just a store, a gas pump, and the post office. Now it is a good-sized town.

We went west of town to Elwert Hibry's. My folks knew them when they first came to the Sandhills. Mrs. Hibry had cooked for Dad's hay camp in 1912, when they put up the Carver hay.

After spending an hour or so there, we went on home.

When we were about two miles north of home, we ran out of gas. Dad had to walk on home to get some. After some time he came back riding a little black horse called

Johnny. All of us kids had learned to ride on him. He was a single-footer and pretty stylish. Mother always rode him. I can see her yet. This is the same horse I rode to Ashby to ship.

After he put the gas in the tank, he said, "Well, here, Franklin, you can ride this horse home."

Mother was pretty put out as I had my good clothes on. She didn't think I was dressed warm enough to ride horseback.

She says, "Where was Bill? Wasn't he home? Why didn't you bring him to ride the horse back?"

Dad laughed and said, "Well, the first reason—he wasn't in a very good humor, and the second reason—I didn't have time to wait for him to change his clothes."

As Dad came up over the hill back of the barn, Bill Kirby had just got on his horse and he bucked him off in the tank. I don't remember where Bill got the horse, but he was a nice black horse. Bill was just breaking him. He was pretty put out to think anyone had seen him get bucked off.

CHAPTER FORTY

Having a New Boyfriend

AFTER CY PORTER left the country, Dad leased his place for several years. There were about 80 acres of farm land on this place. Dad always planted it to corn.

I can remember how he would always mow the outside of the corn field and bunch the hay. After he got the corn picked, he would put his cows in there to clean up the field.

It was always a big day. He would wait until some Saturday in October, then we would go down to the summer range, bunch up the cattle, cut the calves off, and take them home—about six miles. Then, when the cows stopped looking for their calves, we would put them over at the Porter place about a mile away.

Dad would always hire someone to farm this place and pick the corn for him. We had had a real bad winter that year. (It may have been the winter Dad had to leave the car.) Anyway, one Saturday he was going to go down there and get a load of corn.

Vida Hamilton, Franklin Jackson, Nelly Jackson, Carl Jackson.

That morning before he left, he came in while my mother was curling her hair. In those days they had an iron that had wrinkles on one end. She would put that in a coal oil lamp from the top of the chimney, and when it got hot, she would put some of her hair in it to "singe" it curly. Dad wanted to know why she was getting all fixed up.

She said since he was leaving that maybe her boyfriend would come to see her.

Later in the evening there came a fellow on a bob sled buying furs. He wasn't much of a looker and a little old. In those days people didn't get to go to shows much. He had been to a show he thought was pretty good, so he was

75

sitting out in the kitchen telling Mother about this show. He was sitting on the back of his chair, waving his arms, and really going on when Dad came in. He looked him over. (The fellow didn't stop talking.)

Dad walked in the other room and said, "Katy, would you come in here?" She knew what he wanted, but went on in.

Dad says, "Boy, is that all the better you can do?" We never did let Mother forget about her boyfriend.

CHAPTER FORTY-ONE

Moving the Bar Circle Cattle

I DON'T KNOW what year the U-Cross bought the Diemer cattle, but I think it was probably in 1925. I didn't get to go as they went in August and I was herding horses for the hay camp then. I can't remember who the cook was, if Dad ever told me. The cowboys were Dad, Mose Rosseter, Jim Mogle, Dentist Wolford, Vane Hubbard, and Bert Schrader.

They still had to haul all their supplies from town by freight wagon, so they didn't take enough to get to Hyannis. It must have taken them longer on the road than they figured.

They didn't have any breakfast the morning before they got to Hyannis. They camped about ten miles north of town. When they broke camp the next morning, Mose says, "Well, Jim, let's you and I ride on to town and get the supplies bought so we won't have to wait."

Dad said when they went by the hotel, he saw Mose and Jim in the cafe eating breakfast. They had put the groceries out on the sidewalk, so they loaded them up and went on out of town and got breakfast.

They were just getting ready to eat when Jim and Mose rode up. Dad said he guessed Mose didn't want the rest of them to know they had eaten because he got off his horse, grabbed a plate, and went to filling it up.

Jim stood there watching him. He says, "Boy, Mose, how can you eat anymore after the breakfast we just ate?"

Mose surely looked cheap, but didn't say anything. He went ahead and ate.

They got out to the Bar Circle that day. It is where Farrars' ranch is now. The U-Cross had bought all the cattle including the brand. They were there around a week getting the cattle gathered and tallied out.

They took the steers—seven hundred and some head of them up about three miles west of Ashby, where they met the Star Ranch wagon to receive them.

They turned around and went back to the Bar Circle, which was about thirty or forty miles.

Joe Minor and Brass of Brass and Myers were the administrators of the estate. That was the first Dad had ever worked with either one of them.

When they got back to the ranch that night they could see a bunch of cattle coming from the north—around 500 of them—with one man driving them. No one could figure out who it could be.

Brass and Myers were to move on the ranch, but Brass said it could not be his cattle as there weren't enough, and only one rider.

Dad, Joe Minor, and Mr. Brass rode out to see who it was. When they rode by the leader of the cattle, they could see the Brass and Myers' brand on them, which was called a sugar bowl. When they got up to the cowboy, here it was a Negro cowboy by the name of Al Bray. He lived east of Whitman.

Brass says, "Where are the rest of the cattle, Al?"

He answered, "Well, Mr. Brass, me and the rest of the boys had a little argument over north here a ways. They wanted to go east, and I wanted to go south, so I just cut off what I thought was my share and came on south."

The rest of the fellows got in from the east about noon the next day with around a thousand cattle, and there were about six riders. I think Al must have had his share.

Dad said he was really a top hand. He had worked with him before. When they left for the U-Cross the next morning, Bray slipped up beside Dad.

He said, "Mr. Jackson, you all just catch that silver hoss of mine and ride him. I have never seen you as near afoot as you were yesterday. When you get up north of Hyannis, just turn him loose. I will pick him up some time."

Dad said, "Why, I thought maybe you were going to give him to me, Al."

Bray says, "Oh, no, Mr. Jackson, I could not drive those sugar bowl cattle without that silver horse."

Dad said he was really a top horse. He sure appreciated him. He had only two of his own horses along, and the U-Cross was nearly afoot.

The Bar Circle cattle on the move. (Courtesy of Bert Schrader. He said there were over 3000 head of cattle.)

78

Dentist Wolford told me many times they had 1565 head of cows and calves on that drive.

There was a calf in the bunch that didn't have a front leg on one side—not even a shoulder blade. He played out, north of Hyannis, so they just left him.

Musser came along and saw him. When he caught up with them, they were eating dinner. He didn't even have time to eat for bitching about them leaving this calf to starve to death.

When Dad got done eating he walked over, got his rope off his saddle and says, "Well, Logan, you take me back in your car and I will catch your damn calf for you."

They went back. Dad got out on the fender of the car so he could rope the calf. Logan took after it. Dad had thrown three or four times at the calf, but he would go through the loop on account of this leg being gone.

He was going to have one more chance as the calf was getting close to the hills.

He was sitting up there really spurring to get close. He threw and caught him that time. They loaded him in the car and took him on.

Logan has told me this story many times. I would never see him that he wouldn't say, "Say, Franklin, did I ever tell you about the time your dad spurred all the paint off my new Dodge car aroping a calf?"

Of course I would say, "No," just to hear it again.

When they were eating dinner one day, Mose says, "Vane, when you get done eating, will you get the horses?"

Vane says, "You bet, Mose, but will you tell me just one thing? Does that Bert Schrader get the same money around here I do? You always hear, 'Vane do this,' 'Vane do that,' but you never hear, 'Bert do this or that'." Dad sure used to laugh about this when he would tell it.

Just think how much trouble these drugstore cowboys would have nowadays driving 1500 cattle sixty miles or better with just six men.

CHAPTER FORTY-TWO

Some of the Stories and Men at the Ranch

WHEN THEY GOT BACK to the Ranch, they still had a lot of riding to do, and their horses were about done in.

They had two horses at the Ranch, one they called "Rats" and the other "Skunk." They called the one horse "Skunk" because he would pretty near always play out and leave the rider to walk home. Rats was a good horse, but he was just too tired. He played out on Vane the day before, and he had to walk in. This Skunk horse was in his string too.

Mose was in the corral catching horses one morning when Vane came in and said, "Say, Mose, if this outfit has anything but varmints to ride, catch me a horse this morning. I am sure getting tired of walking."

Mose turned around, looked at him, threw down his rope, and started for the house.

Dad said, "Boy, you should have kept your mouth shut that time, Vane. He has gone to get your time."

Vane says, "Do you think so?" He ran over to the gate. Mose was half way to the house. "Say, Mose, while you are up there, just get my time, will you? I guess I don't need a horse this morning."

Dad said Mose spun around like he was coming back to the corral, then went on to the office and got his pay.

This Vane was a fast thinker, and always had something to say.

They tell the story about him in Denver one time in the Depression.

He was always a good dresser, but he was broke. He hadn't had anything to eat for twenty-four hours.

He was walking down the street when a couple fellows stepped up and says, "Mister, would you stake us to a meal? We haven't had anything to eat for over a day."

Vane says, "Sure, boys, I know what it is to be hungry. I have been there myself. Come along."

They went into a restaurant. Vane told the waiter to bring them three of the biggest T-bone steaks they had, as they were sure hungry.

When the steaks came, Vane just went right to work on his. He says, "Now, you boys enjoy your dinner. I have to hurry back to work, as I am a little late."

He got done before they did, and says, "Now, I will go up to pay for this. When I point back here, so the cashier knows who I am paying for, you be sure to let her know."

He walked up to the desk and told the cashier, "Those two fellows back there will pay for this," and handed her the check.

The fellows both waved their hands, and Vane walked out.

He used to laugh and say he didn't know how they came out, but they all three got something to eat.

Then there was another fellow who worked at the Ranch in later years, by the name of Edmunds. I don't know his first name, either, but they called him Trigger, as he always had an answer for everything.

They tell about in '34 when the times were so hard, they started out to hay. Mose says, "Now I don't want any complaint this year. All this equipment is in A-1 shape (none of it had anything done to it, as they didn't have any money to do anything) and these are all good horses."

Mose came along two days later. Trigger was sitting on the corner, not mowing.

Mose drove up. "Well, what the hell is the matter with you, now?"

Trigger said, "Well now, Mose, control yourself. It is a long story. In the first place, this mower is wore out, and if I had any horses that could pull it, the harness wouldn't hold together long enough for them to do it."

Mose just drove off with nothing to say.

81

Dad says he rode over to the Ranch one time to do some telephoning. He was just going out to the barn, when Speck Cone and Mose came riding up. Mose told Speck to put the horses in the barn. He was visiting with Dad. Speck came to the door and asked Mose where to put his horse. Mose says, "Put him in that stall where I always keep him."

Speck says, "There is a freight horse tied in that stall."

Trigger was doing the freighting, hauling the cake around to different places on the Ranch. Mose went stomping off to the barn, saying, "If that freighter had six horses, he would have to have six stalls to tie them in."

Trigger came out of a stall where he was unharnessing one of his horse, saying, "No, he wouldn't on this outfit, Mose, because he wouldn't have enough ropes to tie them with."

Trigger had worked at the Ranch several years. One year when they got done haying, Mose was paying off the men. When he came to Trigger, he says, "Well, Trigger, if I am still running the outfit next year, I would sure like to have you back."

Trigger looked at Mose, never even smiled, and says, "No, Mose, I won't be back next year. I have worked for a cow outfit the last three years, and ate pork. I think I will work for a hog outfit next year, and see if they feed beef."

In the 30s, when we had the itch in our cattle, Dad made arrangements to dip at Lee McDonnell's. We had to trail our cattle over there—about seven miles. Dad, Harry Henderson, and I had taken them over. It was a long day. We took them over and back the same day. We had over 400 cattle.

Mose had some bulls that had really been bad when they dipped, so he asked Dad if he could dip them again.

Mose and Trigger had helped us that day, so they went over east of the Ranch and got the bulls and one cow.

When we were done dipping, Mose sent Trigger to take them back to the pasture, and told him to take the cow up to the Ranch.

Now, Trigger wasn't a very good cowboy. Mose was about half a mile away, when here come Trigger riding back, hollering at him. Mose turned around, and rode clear back to see what he wanted.

When he got up to the fence, Trigger says, "Why, when you are eating supper, Mose, if any of the boys wonder where I am, you tell them I am down east trying to bring that cow home." He turned around and rode off.

Boy, was Mose disgusted!

An early-day Sandhills post office. Mail carrier, Bert Schrader. Hinchley, Nebraska.

CHAPTER FORTY-THREE

Living in the Good Times

MY YOUNGER SISTER, Nelly Adam, wrote an article for *The Nebraska Cattleman* a few years ago about Dad and Mother, and the hardships we all went through.

I didn't feel that way. Maybe every one looks back on their childhood with longing, but I have always wished my children had lived when I did as I think it was a wonderful time.

I hadn't realized it, but I was visiting with Dad a few years before he died. I said, "Dad, it must seem funny to look back over your life and see the changes that have been made."

He said, "Yes, but did you ever stop to think, most of those changes have been in your life time?" I hadn't, but most of those changes have been.

I suppose it was because my Dad was looked up to so, but there never was a kid that was more spoiled by a bunch of cowboys than I was. I could do no wrong as far as the boys at the Ranch were concerned.

Mose used to always say, "You make a friend of a kid and you have a friend for life." He certainly lived up to it because he always was making over some kid and especially me.

I have had fellows argue with me about how much better horses are nowadays, but I say I rode better horses up until I was thirteen years old than I ever have since.

I had three horses in my string—one a horse Mac got from Bill Locy. He was called Shetland. One was the horse they got from Louis Babby—called Old Joe. The other was a horse Mose got from the Trucks boys. He was called Skeeter. He had been used on the race tracks to start race horses. He was a little crazy when he got warmed up, but these other two were top horses in anybody's string. I wish I had one as good now.

I always remember Dad would turn my white horse out in the winter time. He didn't think we needed more than one horse to go to school on.

Just to show how Mose would cater to me . . . .

We got done branding one afternoon. Mose told Dad what to do about some cattle, and sent a couple of men with him. He said he was going to take the rest of the boys and go have a horse round-up to get some more saddle horses.

I got right over to Dad and asked him if I could go with Mose and get my white horse. I sure needed a change of horses.

Dad said, "No." But Mose came over and wanted to know what I wanted. Dad told him. I can still see Mose laugh and say, "Well, come on, Franklin. A fellow sure don't want to be left afoot. That can sure happen if a fellow is short of horses."

We went down in the L Lake country and gathered these horses. When we got to the north side of the pasture, they held the horses against the fence while Mose tried to catch this horse. He had been roped a lot of times and knew how to dodge a rope. Mose had thrown at him four or five times and couldn't catch him.

Mose rode over and asked me what I was going to do with him if he did catch him.

I said, "Ride him."

Mose says, "Fair enough." About that time Dad came. He and Mose ran him between them and Dad caught him.

Boy, as soon as I saw that rope go over his head I was off and started to get the saddle off my horse.

Dad looked up and hollered, "Don't turn that horse loose."

If I had, they would have had a time catching him because he was fast. He was the black horse us kids always rode.

Harry Henderson and Mose Rosseter, and the sign Harry made for Mose.

CHAPTER FORTY-FOUR

Getting Bucked Off and About Branding

THE NEXT MORNING we were branding about six miles east of our ranch. I rode my white horse.

We got about three miles east of the ranch and picked up a cow that had got away from somewhere with an unbranded calf. We started on with her and the calf. She was pretty wild. I can remember how unhappy Dad was. I got bucked off four or five times. Dad would have to catch my horse and then get the cow.

He couldn't understand how a fellow could get bucked off and let his horse get away, but that has always been a failing of mine. I never could hold my horse.

I wasn't as good as Buck Buckles. I furnished the horses for the wild horse race in Merriman a few years back. In the bunch was a black mare.

86

Buck drew her and she bucked him off. Buck held on to her, got back on, and won the race. He said that that is the only time he ever heard of a fellow getting bucked off, getting back on, and still winning the race.

His Uncle Ben said you could sure tell Buck had got bucked off in a big pasture a lot of times, the way he held on to his horse.

It used to be quite a thing in those days when we branded at the Ranch. They would gather the cattle, and pretty soon here would come the big old freight wagon loaded with old posts, and six or eight men on it who never rode horseback.

They would have a couple of fellows with a bunch of loose horses. They would just bunch the cattle on a big flat somewhere, the wagon would drive up, and these fellows would jump off. Two or three would start to dig post holes, and put up a rope corral to run the loose horses in. The others would dig a hole for the fire and get it going. Mose would always holler for Cliff McDonnell, his brother Lewis, and me to start in.

We would always get to catch ten or twelve calves apiece while the irons were getting hot, and Dad and Lee McDonnell were changing horses. We surely thought we were big.

This was just another of the nice things Mose used to do for kids. They always had six sets of wrestlers. Dad and Lee used to keep them busy. I didn't realize how busy, until I got old enough to carry an iron. I used to put the + on, and you really kept in high gear.

In those days they would brand a bunch a day. They always fed 500 cows to a bunch and would brand whatever calves there were in a bunch. In later years they branded two bunches a day.

We three boys always helped hold the herd. I am sure we used to let an unbranded calf or two get away so we could run and catch it.

87

This day when we got started good, there was some fellow taking pictures.

I didn't get to rope that morning, as Dad was afraid I would get in trouble—as much trouble as I had riding to work that morning. I was pretty put out until Logan Musser's boy, Billy—who was there that day, and Mose let him ride my Skeeter horse—roped a calf, and his horse got tangled up, went to bucking, and wrapped Billy up in the rope. Dad and Lee McDonnell were horseback. One grabbed the horse, and the other one got the kid untangled and off the horse.

By that time there were a bunch of the other fellows there, but that is just an example of how those old timers could move, and get where they were needed right now.

When we were going home that night, Dad said, "Now, see why I didn't want you to rope a calf?"

I told him, "Yes." My Dad always had a reason for what he said, if we could just see it.

Carl Jackson, Franklin Jackson, Catherine Jackson, and Nelly Jackson.

CHAPTER FORTY-FIVE

Herding Horses and Killing Time

DAD USED TO PUT UP our hay and stack the valley north of us, belonging to the U-Cross, around 800 or 900 ton altogether.

He was always done by the first of August. Then he would move from home to what was known as the 36, or L Lake country. Then, for the U-Cross, he would mow and bunch with a hay rake around 3500 acres of hay.

At this time, this was all one big pasture. There must have been ten or twelve sections of land in it.

He had a horse corral and small pasture at each camp to put the horses in at night.

Starting when I was about seven years old, I herded the horses in the day time. There were around 75 or 80 head of horses, not counting the colts, of which there were always 20 head or more.

I cannot see how Mother ever got her work done like she did. They always got up at 4 o'clock. She would call me. I would get up, and go saddle my horse. By that time she would have my breakfast ready. I would eat and leave. The one corral was in the 36. I was to have the horses in when the men got there. The other corral was at the west end of what they called Steve Lake. The corral was pretty close to where Dad's house sat, when he owned this place.

The first corral was about four miles from home. The other one about eight or maybe ten miles the way they had to go with the car.

Mother would always take the men to work, wait until Dad was harnessed up and gone. Then she would go home. She and Gladys would get dinner, and she would bring that to the men, go back home, start supper, and come back and get the men. She and Gladys would get supper on while the men washed up for supper.

I was always supposed to put the horses in the small

89

pasture wherever we were haying at the time, at about 4 o'clock, and lope home, and get the cows in. Gladys and I were to have them milked when the men got home.

The days were surely long, and seemed to get awfully hot.

I guess they must not have had polio germs at that time because, as I have told my kids, I don't know why I didn't get it. I used to ride up to the flowing well tank and jump off my horse into that water. It was really cold.

I would go out and lie on the hill somewhere in the sun. When I got dry, I would repeat the process. Pretty near every valley would have a flowing well in it.

Some of those old mares used to get pretty smart about trying to get away. They would graze along some hill, and pretty soon would duck up some draw and really take off.

I would lie and watch them until I thought they had a good start, and then, would I take off after them! That helped to break the monotony.

I can remember one time Mother and Gladys both came to bring the dinner. They had a fellow with them who was walking through the country. I think he must have escaped from some asylum some where. He was surely a queer fellow.

He had come just as Mother was getting ready to leave. Of course she didn't want to leave Gladys alone with him and she didn't want to take him along with her alone, so she had Gladys go along and drive. We have always had a lot of fun with Mother. She sat in the back seat with Dad's six shooter under her apron on this fellow all the way to camp.

Dad kept him there at camp, and took him to town a day or so later.

This fellow had a whole pocket full of newspaper cut up. He said that was oil stock. The boys all called him John D. He would get real mad, and say, "I am not John D. just because I have some oil stock."

CHAPTER FORTY-SIX

It Pays to Wear a Big Hat

THERE WAS A FELLOW lived over northwest of us by the name of Let Beckwith. He had moved to Gordon, leased his place, and got the job of game warden.

Dad had a lake that had a lot of bullheads in it. We always kept a seine to get these fish with. There is a large grove of hackberry trees on the south side of this lake. When they got leafed out, they always had a big fish fry there in the spring. Over a hundred people would come, and they would really have a good time.

I would like to know how many fish were taken out of this lake. I have seen as high as 25 sacks full taken out on a Sunday.

These environmentalists claim that you shouldn't take too many fish out, but this lake was good for years—until it dried up.

The fellow who ran the Survey Post Office, by the name of A. N. Barker, would take up a collection at the store every three or four years to buy a new seine.

We always left it at a certain place in the hills. Everyone knew where it was and would walk to where it was, so there were no roads for any outsiders to see.

Let Beckwith knew about this. He would write Dad a letter saying that he expected to be in the country such and such a time. We would always have things cleaned up for him.

One time, in haying, Dad had a kid driving the stacker who was really a good shot. He used to take a rifle to the field and shoot young grouse.

When he would come by the front gate, he would hand his lines to one of the men, and run in with his grouse. He always tossed them inside the kitchen door, and went on out to help take care of his horses.

We were just coming to the house from the barn one

day, when a car drove up. It was Beckwith and a state game warden. He hadn't been able to let Dad know.

Dad walked out to the car. Let introduced him to the state man and, of course, Dad invited them in to dinner.

This is the only time I ever knew Dad to walk in his door ahead of anyone. But he did. He kicked the grouse in a pile, and threw his hat over them. He invited these fellows on in and showed them where to put their hats. He hurried out to the kitchen, grabbed these grouse, and put them in the pantry. Then he showed the fellows where to wash for dinner. After dinner he walked out to the car with them.

This Beckwith had a nervous condition. His lips would keep going back like he was smiling.

They got in the car ready to go. Beckwith looked up at Dad like he was smiling, and said, "Boy, it surely pays to wear a big hat, doesn't it, Carl?"

Dad never did know if the state man knew what was going on or not.

CHAPTER FORTY-SEVEN

Horses and Handling Them

DAD ALWAYS TRIED to raise 25 draft colts every year. He would break them to work when they were four years old.

Some of the lighter ones he would break to ride when they were three, and break them to work when they were four, as the farmers really liked that kind of horse. They called them dual purpose. He would work them that summer and the next summer, when they were five, and ship them that winter.

He always gave a horse sale at Havelock, a suburb of Lincoln, Nebraska, every winter in February sometime.

I was visiting with Steve Sterns the other day. He was telling about one time when Dad stayed there with a load of horses.

He had sent Sterns word that he would be there at a certain time, so Steve had hauled a load of hay up to the gate of the corral.

When Dad got there, Steve told him they could just harness up a team and haul this hay into the corral. Dad thought they could scatter this hay without harnessing a team.

Steve had a fellow by the name of Cumroy working for him. He was a big man and really stout. He walked out, stuck his fork in this hay, and took a big forkful of it in and scattered it out to the horses. Steve said he and Dad stood, watching the gate and visiting. Then Dad chuckled all the way back to the house about how they got out of harnessing a team.

Dad was a superb horseman. He always had a lot of good pulling horses. I tell people I was sixteen or seventeen years of age before I knew there was anything a horse couldn't pull.

Dad had a black team we kids had learned to drive with. He always worked them on the stacker. In those days, if they had a man or kid they couldn't use anywhere else, they put him on the stacker cart. This old team had had so many of this kind of driver, they would balk if the going got tough just to try out the driver.

Dad used to like to tell about one time when he had a kid from Tennessee working and driving the stacker. Dad and Gladys were sweeping. It was getting pretty close to quitting time. They had pulled across the creek, and he told the kid to pull across when he was ready. They wanted to get up another stack if they could. Dad always said there were few men that could pull a line as good as Gladys. This kid got stuck in the creek and the old black team would not pull for him.

93

Dad asked Gladys if she thought she could pull the stacker out.

"Sure, Dad," she said. She drove up to where the kid was stuck, got off her sweep, walked over, gathered up the lines, straightened the team out, pulled back her line, and laid it across those horses.

Dad used to say how he could see the hair fly clear from where he was—a quarter of a mile away. They really pulled the stacker out.

I would like to know how many miles my younger sister and I rode with Dad gathering up horses.

I don't know yet how we could do the things we did. Dad would gather up a bunch of horses, maybe 200 head. He would put them up against a fence somewhere and have us hold them while he would cut out what he wanted. Then we would go on.

I can remember one time when he bought twenty head of mules, and seven of those mules were still sucking the mares. We just went down, cut the mules off, and took them home. It was about fourteen miles from home.

Anybody who has ever handled mules knows this must have been quite an accomplishment. That is what I mean about riding good horses. I was eight years old at this time and there was just Dad and me.

CHAPTER FORTY-EIGHT

The First Long Cattle Drive and Stock People

I THINK IT MUST HAVE BEEN in about 1925, when the Gordon State Bank closed out Mrs. Julia Braddock. They wintered the cattle at Houston Waddills' that winter and sold them to Card and Adams.

Frank Card had bought a place north of Ashby. He wanted these cows and calves taken to this ranch. It was about sixty miles. Lawrence Bixby had recommended Dad for the job, so Card had contacted Dad, and he agreed to do it. There were Dad, Frank Hamilton, Shorty Prindle, and I.

We went to Irwin in one day, which was probably about 35 or 40 miles straight across. I can hear Dad "cuss" yet, because as we came over the big hill south of Irwin, they were just penning the cattle. We were in a wagon and had our extra horses tied on the side. The cattle were supposed to be ready to go when we got there.

I can remember that while we were setting up the tent, Card came up and gave Dad a cigar and was telling him about how much trouble they had had. That is the one and only time I ever saw my Dad smoke. I guess maybe he was so mad he thought this might cool him off.

The next day they worked all day and didn't get much done. They had to get all the papers straightened out. Half of these cattle were to be shipped East somewhere.

That evening Fay Hill told Card that if he wanted to pay Mrs. Braddock, he thought she could probably help them out a lot. Card told him to get her.

I can remember how they came with her the next morning. They went up the hill and got a big chair with arms on it from the store. I don't suppose Mrs. Braddock was too old at this time, but she seemed real old to a kid like me. They set this chair down, put a board across the arms of it, and piled these papers on it.

She sat there all day. There was never a cow that got up to the end of the chute that she didn't have the papers ready for her.

These were all purebred cows. They had to re-horn-brand and see that the papers were there for each cow.

This always stuck in my mind—what a stockperson she must have been. I have always regretted that I didn't go to visit her when we lived at Wood Lake. She lived in Bassett.

She lost her life while going out to her ranch south of Bassett in a snow storm.

Another event that always stuck in my mind happened at the school house set west of the stockyards. They had to take the horses out and back by there every night and morning.

Hap Sterns was going on the Card place for Card. He was just a young fellow—got married that spring—and Shorty Prindle was a single fellow. They had got to talking about the teacher and Shorty thought he would like to see what she looked like. So one afternoon when Hap was taking the horses back, he told Shorty to get where he could see her, as he was going to bring her out.

Shorty got out on a knoll, from the tent aways. When Hap went by the school house, he let out a yell and roped the stove pipe. It really made a noise as it came bouncing off the roof.

The teacher and all the kids came running out to see what all the commotion was about.

When he came back, Hap asked Shorty if he had seen the teacher. Shorty laughed and said he hadn't, that he could tell she was mad. He didn't want her to think he was involved, so he didn't watch.

When we got down to Card's, I was riding my white horse. Card surely fell for him. He asked me what I would take for him as his boy was coming out that summer to the ranch. He would surely like to have a horse like him for the boy to ride.

Of course I didn't know anything about money. I told him $100 (which would have been a big price). He said he would just buy him. Of course I didn't want to lose my horse, and I said, "I mean $300."

Card always had to tell this on me to show what a poor horsetrader I was.

He gave Dad some money to buy me a new hat though, so I thought he was a pretty nice guy.

CHAPTER FORTY-NINE
School Teachers and Diplomas

DURING MY THIRD YEAR of school Frank Hamilton was
the director on the school board. He had no car. The only
way he had of contacting a teacher was through the mail. I
suppose, as he had no children going to school, he wasn't
too concerned about the lack of a teacher. Anyway, it was
time for school to start, and he didn't have a teacher yet.

He told Dad to go ahead and hire a teacher if he could
find one. Dad went to Gordon on a Sunday afternoon to
see if he could get one. He went into Emery Potts's cafe to
eat supper. There was a girl working in there by the name
of Ruth Lefler. She was a sister to the fellow who wouldn't
stay fired at the Overton.

Dad asked her if she was interested in teaching school.
She told him she had just hired out that day, but she knew
a girl who had just graduated from high school that spring
and would sure like to get a school. Her name was Phoebe
Hawk. She hadn't passed her teacher's exams yet, but she
was surely working on them. She was supposed to take
them in a short time.

Dad went out to see her. She was a country girl and
lived out south of town. Dad hired her, and we started
school the next day.

In a short time he got a letter from the County Superintendent saying that they could not acknowledge a teacher
without a certificate. Roy Dille was the treasurer of the
district. Dad went to him and told him to draw out all the
county funds they had for the district, and they would just
go on having school.

Roy did this. In a short time Dad got a letter from the
State Superintendent, telling Dad what they were going to
have to do and what they couldn't do.

Dad was not much of a hand to write a letter, but I can
see him yet, sitting there and writing this letter. He told

97

the State Superintendent that he always thought it would be nice to be able to sit in a nice warm office, with your feet on a desk, laying down rules for what someone had to do, or not do, but he knew from experience it was awfully hard to sit at that desk, with your feet up, and see that they did it. He signed this letter and mailed it.

A short time later they were dipping over at the Ranch. After dinner Dad went over and sat down beside Logan Musser. He asked him how well he knew the County Superintendent in Rushville—that is where this girl had to pass her examinations.

Logan held up his hand with his fingers crossed, and says, "We are just like that, Carl. What is your problem?" Dad told him. Logan says, "Think no more about it." In about a week the girl's certificate came in the mail.

When Gladys was just starting school, the folks had hired a teacher, but she quit in a short time.

Teacher, Eve Skelton, Harry Henderson, Carl Jackson, Franklin Jackson, Nelly Jackson, and Fred Grover, taken the winter of 1936.

The County Superintendent came out to see about the school. She asked Mother why she didn't teach it. Mother said that she wasn't a teacher and didn't have a certificate. The County Superintendent says, "Why, you went to school, didn't you?"

Mother told her she had had one year of high school.

"Well, here then," she said, sat down, wrote out about twenty questions, and told Mother to answer them. When Mother did, the Superintendent signed a paper and said, "Here is your permit."

Mother finished the school year. I can't see but what we did about as well as, or maybe a lot better, than kids do in school today.

We never did have but eight months of school a year, and as I said earlier, the first two years I went only about eleven months altogether. Eight of us children graduated from the eighth grade, from that little white school house, and I can't see but what we have all done real well. I have always thought we got more education from those eight grades than these children do now from high school.

I have always been a firm believer that it wasn't what you knew, but who you knew anyway.

CHAPTER FIFTY

Getting a Free Ride

I DON'T REMEMBER what year it was, but some fellows from Omaha had leased the hunting on Gourley's place. They had built a real nice camp house, and a bunch of them would come out and spend about ten days hunting.

I think this was in about 1928. The first year they came they brought a Negro cook with them. I surely thought he was a good fellow, as he made a deal with me to rent my saddle horse every afternoon to ride and take pictures in the hills. It was only about a mile from the school house. He gave me 25¢ a day for the use of him.

The road went right by this camp house going to the post office. One day Dad stopped and asked him if he would like to ride along with him to the post office.

The Negro mixed them a drink before they left, as he told Dad the hunters had told him when any of the fellows came to be sure to treat them. When they got back from the post office, they had another drink. The Negro got to telling Dad what a good revolver shot he was.

Dad told him he was a good shot, too. The fellow went and got his gun, put some bottles up on the fence posts, and decided to see who could shoot the most off.

He told Dad he always liked to have some kind of a wager to make it more interesting.

There was a boat trailer sitting there. Dad told him, "All right, we will shoot. The one that gets the most bottles, the other one has to give him a ride in this trailer up to the flowing well." The well was half a mile up the valley.

It was really sandy all the way. The Negro shot first and got five bottles. Dad shot and got all six bottles, so the fellow had to give him a ride.

Dad said he would pull aways, and then have to rest. When they were coming back, the fellow says, "You know, I am a better knife man than I is a shot."

Dad said, "Oh, I am really good with a knife, too."

When they got back the fellow went in and Dad said he came out with about as wicked-looking a knife as he had ever seen.

Dad always was an excellent shot but, as near as I know, he hadn't thrown a knife in his life.

The Negro said, "Now, Mr. Jackson, you see that crack in the door. Well, we will both throw at that crack. The one that comes the closest, the other one has to pull him up to that well and, Mr. Jackson, I is sure goin' to enjoy that ride."

He stepped off where they agreed to throw from, and let go. The knife just cut a small sliver off beside the crack in the door. He really was tickled. He thought Dad had just as well give him the ride as he couldn't beat that.

Dad stepped off the mark, let fly, and, Surprise! He said the knife went right in the crack. He got another ride. Of course, it took quite a while to make the trip that time. The Negro had to take a few drinks along as he didn't know if he could make it or not the second time.

While they were making the trip, he was telling Dad how these hunters really looked down on him, and what a good fellow he thought Dad was to associate with him and show him such a good time.

Dad told him he shouldn't take anything off of those hunters, because, out here, we always thought everyone was the same.

So, when the hunters got back that night the fellow just ran them off. Of course, I suppose he was getting a little high anyway, but they had to go somewhere else to stay all night.

I can remember the next fall when the hunters came, Mr. Morrison stopped and told Mother to tell Dad he wanted him to stay away that year, as they had a new cook, and he had orders not to associate with the people in the community. They all had a good laugh about it.

CHAPTER FIFTY-ONE

Building a Shed and More House

I THINK IT WAS IN 1926 when Dad decided to build a new shed and put two more rooms on the house.

My sister and I really thought that was great—to have more bedrooms. We had had only a four-room house.

Dad had to freight all this lumber from Gordon, which

was a three-day trip. They used six head of horses to the wagon. I don't remember how many trips it took, but the shed was thirty by eighty. It was all made of lumber, even wooden shingles. The sides were ten feet high. This shed still stands today and is in use by the Runners.

My sister Gladys graduated from high school in 1928, and had a teacher's certificate. She taught school one year, then married Bert Jensen. They had two boys. One of them was killed in a car accident. My grandfather Jackson died in 1929; my grandfather Mahoney in 1924. I married Elsie Lee King in 1940 and have five children.

My younger sister was married in 1946 to Wallace Adam. They have three boys. My younger brother married Mary Sandoz in 1952. They had one boy and later parted. He married Evelyn Beiler in 1956. They have two boys and two girls.

My grandmother Mahoney passed away in 1933 and my grandmother Jackson in 1958. My wife's father, Lee D. King, passed away in 1964; her mother, whose maiden name was Calame, died in 1969. They had both homesteaded in the Sandhills.

Elsie Calame taught school before she was married. She taught at the U-Cross once and rode from her homestead—about six miles—horseback to school at that time.

The times were starting to change. Dad bought a tractor with dual mowers in 1929. It was the first one in that part of the country, outside of the one Chris Abbott got the same year.

Dad put up the U-Cross hay one more year, and then they put up all their hay themselves for a good many years, as the times were so hard.

Dad closed out all his horses, but one stallion, ten brood mares, and four work geldings in the winter of '31 and '32. He sold his tractor in '32 and didn't get another until 1940.

My brother, Jerry, was born in 1931.

Dad ran his last freight wagon in 1933.

He and Harry Henderson hauled twenty ton of cake that fall with horses from Gordon. I remember an experience they had. They hauled their water with them in a five-gallon wooden keg for their own use. They kept talking about how funny the water tasted. One day when they were camped for noon, they went to make their coffee. As they were pouring out the water, here came part of a mouse out. He had got in the keg some way. Needless to say, they never used any more water out of that keg.

Turpin Lake School, 1929/30. Left to right: Elsie Dille, Nelly Jackson, Winnie Henderson, Daisy Dille, Franklin Jackson, Walter Harms, Irene Dille and Arthur Dille, and the teacher's car.

CHAPTER FIFTY-TWO

Hard Times and Finances

TIMES REALLY GOT HARD. My Mother still has the papers to show that they shipped sixty head of two-year-old heifers in 1934 for $750 net for the bunch. A lot of these young people don't realize cattle were ever that cheap.

Dad went to Gordon and then to Omaha with Logan Musser on a pass they had when shipping cattle.

If I am not mistaken, the Fawn Lake Cattle Company was doing business with a company known as the Intermediate Trust Company.

Dad was dealing with the Regional, a government loan company.

Logan came to get Dad to go to dinner the first day. While they were eating dinner, he asked Dad how he was getting along. Dad said that he wasn't sure, and asked Logan how he was getting along.

Logan said he wasn't, but he says, "I am going to right after dinner. Come along, and I will show you how this is done."

After dinner they went up to Logan's loan office, and walked in. Dad said he had never seen so many stenographers in an office in his life. Logan walked right across the room toward a door.

There was a little fellow with a white shirt and necktie working at a desk. He saw them coming. He jumped up in front of Logan and says, "Oh, Mr. Musser, you can't go in there now. They are holding a meeting on your problem now."

Logan says, "Good."

Logan was a big man. He reached out and grabbed this fellow by the shirt and his necktie, set him to one side, opened the door, and walked in. Dad said he was right

104

behind him because he didn't know if he could set this fellow out of his road or not.

There were about ten fellows sitting at a desk in conference in this room. The fellow at the head of the desk saw Logan, jumped up, and says, "Oh, Mr. Musser, you can't come in here now. We are on your problem right now."

Logan says, "Good, that is what I want. I just came in to tell you I have ten thousand head of cattle out there on the range and fifteen cowboys waiting word from me on where to go with them. I can sell my hay for a good price. Where do you want the cattle?"

Oh, my, they couldn't handle that many cattle!

One fellow says, "Why, Mr. Musser, what would you have to have to keep in business?"

Dad said Logan really made it tough. He needed two brand new Ford trucks, one carload of coal, and I don't remember how many tons of cake.

This fellow says, "I don't see why we can't do that." Logan turned around and walked out. He spoke to the fellow at the desk as he went by.

Dad said he guessed it paid to get belligerent with those money fellows as he could remember after World War I, money was real tight. Some fellows had made arrangements for a bunch of New York bankers to meet with them in Omaha.

Mac took Dad back with him.

There was a fellow by the name of John Bachelor there too. John was pretty plain spoken. The other ranchers decided maybe he shouldn't go to the meeting. He might spoil things for them.

Mac told Dad to keep him entertained and keep him from the meeting.

Dad and John went to supper and back to their hotel room. Every once in a while John would say, "Is it time

105

for that meeting? We sure don't want to miss that meeting."

Dad kept stalling him. Finally John just got off the bed, pulled on his boots, and says, "Come on, young fellow. I know it is time for that meeting."

When they got to the meeting, Dad said John just walked right in, spitting tobacco juice and cussing. "What do you so-an-sos mean having this meeting without me? I am one of the biggest cattlemen in Western Nebraska."

When Dad saw Mac, he told him he just couldn't keep him away any longer. Mac laughed and said, "John got more done in fifteen minutes than we had been able to get done in one hour."

Frank Jackson and Nellie Pogason Jackson, seated. Bess Jackson, Carl Jackson, and Ruth Jackson, standing. 1928.

CHAPTER FIFTY-THREE

Bosses and Work

IN 1937 MOTHER MOVED TO TOWN to send my youngest sister to high school and to start my little brother in school, as they had shut down the little white school house that spring, the first time since it had been built.

My sister and two Dille girls had taken a high school course for three years from the University of Nebraska. There were no other children left in the district except for my brother.

Dad and I batched that winter at home. About the first of November a buddy of mine, Fred Grover, who had worked for us in haying a number of years, came home, so he did the cooking. He was a good cook, too.

We were dipping over at the Ranch. Dad always had to be the first man on a job. It didn't make any difference if you got any sleep or not. Fred and I sure didn't get much there for about ten days.

We had just got in the boiler house one morning, when John Van Ausdale, who was firing the boiler, says, "Boy, things aren't going to be good around here this morning."

Dad asked him why.

"Well, we had a pretty tough poker game last night, and I overslept. I saw the light come on in the office just as I left this morning."

Mose came in just then. "Is the dip hot, John?"

"You bet."

"Well, let's see."

John took his testing can and went out to get some dip.

As soon as he went out, Mose says, "He will get that right under the spout."

107

John came in. The dip was just right. Mose asked him where he got it. John told him he got it at the other end of the vat. Mose grabbed the can, went out and got some dip, and came in and tested it. It was about two degrees too hot.

"All right. Let's go, boys."

Fred and I grabbed our shillelaghs and went out. There weren't any of the rest of the boys there yet. We were trying to get some cattle in the alley when Mose came out and says, "Where the hell is everyone?" I told him I didn't think anyone else was there yet. You could just see Clyde Lefler coming along the east side of the corral against the horizon. He was taller than any of the rest of the boys. (He was a brother of the boy at the Overton.)

Boy, did Mose air them out good!

When we went home that night here was a fellow by the name of Lawrence Groves looking for a job. Dad told him if he wanted to go with us the next morning, he was sure he could get him a job at the Ranch.

Well, we hadn't much more than got there the next morning when the boys came horseback just as hard as their horses could run. It is four miles from the ranch to the vat, and the boys had outrun Mose. He didn't realize what they were doing until he was about a quarter mile from the vat. He really stepped on the gas, but they beat him.

Lefler was in the lead. He came in just as hard as his horse could run, stepped off, and says, "Boy, I guess I am going to have to find me another place to work. Anything I hate is to get to work and not have a boss around to tell me what to do."

Mose stepped out of his pickup and says, "Well, get your horses, and let's go."

We had to cut a bunch of two-year-old heifers off some cows before we could dip this morning.

108

We sat there around the herd, and it was so dark you couldn't even see your horse's ears.

When we got home that night Dad asked Lawrence if he asked Mose for a job. He said, "No, Sir. I know I am not good enough to hold down a job there."

Mose was not a bad fellow to work for. I don't think there are many men who ever worked there that didn't like him. Another wonderful thing about Mose was that whenever there was a bad storm, he always sent two men together.

He had sent two fellows up to White Valley to feed. It was really bad. When these fellows got done feeding, they just went over to Lawrence Macumber's and stayed all night. He lived right by where they fed.

After supper Mose got about seven or eight of the boys out and they rode up to see why they hadn't come home. It was about seven or eight miles up there. They rode up to Macumber's. Mose hollered at the boys to see if they were there. One of them answered and said, "Boy, it sure is a tough storm, isn't it, Mose?"

Mose says, "Hell, I have picked tomatoes in worse weather than this." He walked out, got on his horse, and went to the Ranch.

That is just the way Mose always looked after his men.

Mose always had Fred and me work in the alley. He said we could put more cattle up the alley with less trouble than anyone else. We had had a cow one morning that didn't want to go up the alley to the vat. Rather than keep crowding her, we just let her back, thinking she would go after a while. That evening, when she was the last one, we were trying to get her up. She got on the fight. Jim Mogle came back, took the prod pole from Clyde Kime, and jumped over in the crowding pen. Every time she turned around, he would stick this electric prod on her.

109

When the cattle would slow up, Mose always hollered, "More cattle. More cattle."

Finally he came back, saw what Jim was doing, and says, "I have told you fellows not to use those prods in that crowding pen." He jumped over the fence, threw up his arms, and hollered. The cow really went up the alley. Mose turned around, crawled over the fence, saying, "See, you don't need those prods."

Mogle waited until he was out of hearing, and says, "Now, if that isn't the way it goes. Get something about ready to go. He comes along and takes the credit. I wonder if he ever stopped to think I taught him all he knows about the cattle business, and kept back the best part." We sure used to have a good laugh about this, as Mose and Jim had worked on the T O when Mose was just a kid.

CHAPTER FIFTY-FOUR

Practical Jokes

I SUPPOSE EVERYONE has some year that sticks out in their life more than others, but the winter of '37 and '38 is mine.

Along in February Dad went to Gordon and took the family back to school. He forgot to come back for about three weeks.

Fred and I surely had a ball. We were young and full of life. We would get up early. I would do the chores while Fred got breakfast. Then we would go feed. We were always done by 8:30 or 9:00 o'clock, so we had the rest of the day to play in.

Harry and Ruth Henderson had come back to her folk's (Dave Gourley's) place that winter. They had been working at the U-Cross. Harry was feeding in the valley in front of our house.

When we got done feeding, we would go and feed his hay out, then load up for the next day.

He came over one day, drank coffee, and gave us some static about us not loading a big enough load or something. Well, Dad had a little sled. It was about six by eight feet, and we used it to clean out the barn and shed with. We got up the next morning, took this little sled over, loaded all the hay we could pitch on it, and pulled it right up in front of his sled so he would have to take it out before he could get through the gate with his load. Then we went home and sat and watched him.

He had something to crab about when he came over for coffee that day.

He sure got even with me though. Fred left along in March, when Dad came home.

It was a nice day along in April. Dad and I had gone down east about two miles, fed our cattle, and had torn down a stack yard. We cut out some dry cattle and took them up west about three miles. When we were coming back to get dinner, here came a fellow from over west by the name of Earl Bestol. While we were sitting there talking, about ten cars came by across the valley going east.

Earl wondered where they could all be going. Dad thought down to the big lakes to get some carp. Earl thought he could sure go for some fish.

Dad told him if he wanted to come over for dinner, we would go over north and get some bullheads.

After dinner we got our seine and rode through the hills. We made one drag and got so many fish we couldn't even get them out on the land. Earl thought he would go home, get his pickup, and haul a lot of these fish over and put them in his stock tank.

We always kidded him, saying that he had been there on this place all winter and nobody had ever seen him ride

111

his horse off a walk. He got about a half mile up the valley, jumped his horse into a lope, and loped clear out of sight. We told him we thought it was a heck of a note to shock his horse that way, just over a few fish. Dad told me to go get our pickup and we would take a load of them, too.

We had left our pickup truck down where we had fed that morning. I loped down to get it and met Harry Henderson about a fourth of a mile from it. He stopped and visited awhile. I thought he acted real funny, but couldn't figure out why.

When I got to our pickup, I could see why. He had jacked it up and piled fence posts under it until it was a good three feet off the ground.

I hope he had to work as hard to get them under there as I had to to get them out.

Dad was very unhappy when I got back. He couldn't figure out why I was gone so long.

It was a good thing we got those fish when we did because the pelicans came the next week and cleaned them out.

Just to show what kind of a fellow Harry was . . . . He was working at the U-Cross, and Ruth was living on the creek west of us where they had lived for several years. There was a fellow by the name of Oscar Hunter working at the Ranch who was really stuck on the hired girl. Afterwards he married her.

He used to stay up at the house after supper and help her with the dishes. The other fellows always were in bed when he came back to the bunk house, so they decided it would be a good joke to pull a trick on him.

They gathered a bunch of tin cans, tied them to the door so they would really make a racket when the door was opened. Then they hung a bucket of water over the door so that when it was opened, it would fall on him.

When he came in, the bucket of water turned over right on his head, and the other cans really made a commotion.

When he finally got the bucket off his head, he just stood there and cussed Henderson. The boys really lay there and laughed because Harry had gone home that night after supper, so he was plumb innocent. That is just an example of how he was usually the instigator of things.

Catherine Jackson, Ruth Henderson, and Harry Henderson.

CHAPTER FIFTY-FIVE

Neighbors and Ranch Operations

THE ROSSETERS WERE great neighbors and friends to the folks. I remember how Mother used to tell about how John Van Ausdale would always come by if he was any-where in the locality and get some pickles from Mother. She used to put her cucumbers up in some salt brine in the summer in a thirty-gallon crock jar. Then she would make pickles as she needed them in the winter. But it had been a tough winter and she had run out of vinegar.

We hadn't been to town to get any vinegar, so when John stopped to get some pickles, Mother didn't have any. She told him she was out of vinegar.

The next day, here came Clyde Rosseter on a bob sled. He came in and said, "Mrs. Jackson, you know you are welcome to anything you need from the ranch, but what is so necessary about vinegar?"

Seated: Shirley King Ostrander, Thelma King, Elsie King, and Lee King. Standing: Elsie Lee King Jackson, Kenneth King, Virgil King, Sophia King Anderson, Eugene King, Myrtle King Blaylock, and Phyllis King. 1947

He had brought her a gallon of vinegar. After John left the day before, he rode by the Ranch and told Clyde that Mrs. Jackson was out of vinegar and surely needed some.

Here Clyde had harnessed a team and driven six miles though deep snow to bring her a gallon of vinegar.

One time Musser came over to Dad's. Dad thought Musser and Mose must have had a little trouble that

114

morning because, after visiting some time, he said, "Carl, how does that Mose keep any help around at all?"

Dad told him to ask John, who was with Logan. "He has worked there a long time."

John said, "Well, there isn't a ranch in the West sets as good a table as the U-Cross. When a man has his stomach full, he can take a lot of abuse...." But Mose was well liked, and always had a good crew of men.

One fellow by the name of Chuck Goedde worked there a long time. I have heard him say several times since that if he knew any place he could go and work with as good a bunch of fellows and ride the same kind of horses he had at the U-Cross, he would go there and work for nothing for a year, just to be with a bunch like that again.

CHAPTER FIFTY-SIX

My Folks and Other People as Neighbors

THE FOLKS REALLY LIVED for good fellowship. It may have been the times and conditions the folks had always been under, but they were always the first people any-where if someone needed some help. They taught us children the same.

I can remember one time a fellow drowned in a dam east of our place. I suppose there were a hundred people there to help get the body out. They had to wait until they brought a seine from Valentine to drag him out. It was about 100 miles the way the road was.

About 12:30, Mother came with a big pressure cooker full of stew and a lot of coffee and fed everyone. She laughed when she passed it out, and said it wasn't much, but it would tide them over until they got something better.

115

It didn't make any difference how busy Dad was, we children always knew he had time to help us with our problems.

Wherever I go, where there is a bunch of people, someone usually brings up my folks and tells of some instance when they did something special for them or someone else.

We certainly lived in a wonderful community in the '30s when times were so hard. They used to have card parties at different places, about every Saturday night in the winter. They would play cards until midnight, eat supper, then dance until daylight. Everyone really had a wonderful time.

My sister wrote in *The Nebraska Cattleman* a few years back about the folks, and how Dad had roped a calf that was a little on the fight. He let this calf take after Mother—hollering, "Look out, Katy, I can't hold him."

She ran and rolled under the fence. When she straightened up, there was Dad sitting on his horse laughing at her. She was pretty put out. Alvie Hamilton told me after he read this article that she had his full sympathy, as Dad had pulled the same trick on him one time.

I guess maybe I kind of evened it up for them one time. I came home from school one night. Dad met me; he was carrying a saw, and said, "We will just dehorn that heifer we missed when we dehorned." We drove her over to a corral.

He roped her by the neck, and I picked up her hind legs. Dad got off, cut off her horns, took his rope off, and said, "Now you hold her till I shut the gate."

I let her have some slack. She got up. The rope came off. I guess she hadn't approved of the treatment she had had, so she took after Dad.

He made about two circles around the corral. Boy, was I laughing! The last time he came around he said, "Get that

116

gate shut! There isn't anything so damn funny." I shut the gate, but still thought it was a pretty good joke.

Bill Louks passed away in 1951. As I sat in the church, looking over the people, I couldn't help but think that I could remember some special time Bill had done something for most of the people there, and how he would be missed.

We gave a celebration for the folks' fiftieth wedding anniversary in 1958. There were over 250 people there. We gave a barbecue, and everyone surely had a good time.

Seated: Carl Jackson, Jerry Jackson, and Catherine Jackson. Standing: Gladys Jackson Jensen, Franklin Jackson, and Nelly Jackson Adam, 1945.

CHAPTER FIFTY-SEVEN

Changing Ranches and the Success of a Man's Life

DAD SOLD THE OLD PLACE at home in 1946. He went to Oregon to visit his mother and relatives there, and to look for a new location.

My brother laughed when they got back. He said going out Dad just drove along enjoying the scenery, and everything on the road passed him.

Dad had a new Ford pickup. He said when Dad got that pickup headed home, the closer he got to Nebraska the faster he went.

When they came across Colorado, Dad was passing everything, including the new Kayser-Frazier cars that had just come out about that time.

He came back and bought the Lee McDonnell ranch. As long as I can remember he always said that was the best ranch he knew of.

I always thought if a man could end up owning what he thought was the best, he had made a great success of his life.

I mentioned this to Reverend DeWitt, the minister for Dad's funeral, one time. He said, "Yes. But I would think that when you saw how many people were at his funeral, and how many tears there were, he must have been a success in another way, too."

My Mother had spent three and a half years in Gordon with my brother when he was in high school.

Dad had just taken them back to town when the 1949 blizzard hit. He and Mose Rosseter spent most of the blizzard together consoling each other.

They had agreed that as soon as an airplane could fly, they would go to their ranches. Dad would go first, as Mose had fellows at his ranch, but Dad had no one at his place.

118

The storm started Sunday evening. They couldn't fly until Wednesday afternoon. Mother, of course, kept worrying about what their loss would be.

Dad said, "Oh, I figure a hundred head."

She said, "Oh, we can't afford that."

He said, "Well, we lost half of them once, and got all right. We are in better shape now than we were then. So I guess we can stand it."

He was running about 400 head at this time and lost three head.

He used to tell about when they flew to the ranch and landed out in the valley. He guessed it was probably that he was walking on the white snow, but when his horses saw him they really took off. Of course all the fences were covered up, and he thought, "Oh, what a time to be afoot!" But one horse ran over some feed bunks. When he went off the other side, he flipped over. The other horses stopped to see what had happened to him. Dad got to the barn by then and had a can of grain. He called them back.

Oats are a great thing for horses that are used to them because you can pretty near always catch one with them.

CHAPTER FIFTY-EIGHT

Moving to Town

MY BROTHER JERRY was not interested in ranching. He left Dad's ranch in 1962 and went to the Virgin Islands. Dad sold his cattle that fall—all but 117 head of heifer calves. He sold the ranch that winter and moved to town.

The next fall he brought the heifers up to my place. It must have been around seventy miles. Dad was 74 years of age and rode all the way horseback.

We gave another get-together in town for the folks' fifty-fifth anniversary the fall of 1963.

That was the last time I saw Mose alive. I can see him and Dad yet, as Mose and his wife came up the walk. Dad shook hands with Mose. You could just see the friendship in their eyes, as they greeted each other.

I was always so thankful the folks both got to travel as much as they did. They went to Cuba once and to the Virgin Islands once to see my brother. They always came back telling of the sights they had seen, and what they had done.

Of course, Dad would always end up telling about the cattle or horses they had seen, and how they took care of them in different places.

Catherine and Carl Jackson, about 1962.

Dad sold the last of his cattle in 1967, so that was the end of an era in his life.

Dad had a stroke in the spring of 1971 and was never the same again. He and Mother went to spend the last days with my sister at Hyannis that fall.

Dad passed away just a few days before his eighty-third birthday at the Mullen Hospital.

We brought him back to put him to rest in the Gordon Cemetery. Mother still lives in Gordon.

I think their lives would be a story for some of these young people today, as Dad was nineteen and Mother was sixteen when they were married. All the hardships they went through and, yet, the great love they had for each other and for their family and friends.

Dean Jensen, Carl Jackson, and Dwight Jensen, 1968. Dad laughed and said he couldn't understand why they let these two fellows stand on a rock when he saw this picture.

From the *Grant County News,* 1972

DEAR JOHN

Last night when Charles and I returned from Carl Jackson's funeral, I felt compelled to write a tribute to this old Cowboy friend of our family.

My mother, daughter of a Methodist Minister and Physician, taught the Kincaiders' children for 7 years. It was Carl Jackson who introduced my dad to my mother at Survey Valley.

Tribute to Carl Jackson

I would like to pay tribute to Carl Jackson and all the old Cowboy settlers who lived and died and are now part of the pioneer history of this vast rolling Sandhill country.

I remember the first time I met Carl Jackson. I was quite young. My brothers and sisters and I loved to roam the hills, playing in the blowouts and building our castles out of sand.

We stopped at a windmill for a cold drink of water. As we turned to leave two cowboys rode up to the mill. I think what stands foremost in my memory were those tall black hats of father and son. I later learned these hats were the trademark of the Jackson men. Never in the years that followed and the close friendship that developed did I ever see Carl Jackson without his tall black hat.

The older cowboy asked our names. When I explained we were Lee and Elsie King's children, he said, "Now you run on home and tell your folks you just met their old

122

neighbors from Survey Valley." I couldn't have been more excited had I just met the President of the United States!

One by one these old cowboys are passing from our sight. They were as hard and as tough as the grains of sand that swept across the tall grass of the range they rode. But in their hearts were the qualities that stand for true manhood: kindness, gentleness, honesty, and neighborliness. Neighborliness was the code of the hills. Neighborliness was the characteristic that made Carl Jackson stand out a man among men. He was a man who loved his fellow men.

A new era has dawned. Progress can no longer be held back. Airplanes and flashy cars have replaced the old freight wagons and buggys. Beautiful oiled highways and REA lines now thread their way across the rolling hills. New generations now live on this land.

Progress is here but in the process something precious has been lost. But somehow I like to think that something of that pioneer spirit is still here with us; that somehow it lingers on in the hearts and souls of those who are left to inherit their land.

Mrs. Charles Blaylock

123

Elsie Lee Jackson and Franklin C. Jackson

About the author

Franklin C. Jackson has lived all his life in the Sandhills area of Nebraska and in nearby South Dakota. He was born in 1917 in Gordon, Nebraska, and grew up on his father's ranch nearby. In 1940, he married Elsie Lee King, of Cherry County. They have five children, four girls and one boy. The Jacksons now live on a ranch near Martin, South Dakota.

This, his first book, is the real story of a pioneering family and of growing up at the end of an era in the American West.